A SHORT INTRODUCTION to
the ANCIENT GREEK THEATER

A SHORT INTRODUCTION *to*

the ANCIENT GREEK THEATER

REVISED EDITION

Graham Ley

The University of Chicago Press
Chicago & London

The University of Chicago Press, Chicago 60637
The University of Chicago Press, Ltd., London
© 1991, 2006 by The University of Chicago
All rights reserved. Originally published in 1991
Revised edition published 2006
Printed in the United States of America

15 14 13 12 11   2 3 4 5

ISBN-13: 978-0-226-47762-6   (cloth)
ISBN-13: 978-0-226-47761-9   (paper)
ISBN-10: 0-226-47762-2   (cloth)
ISBN-10: 0-226-47761-4   (paper)

Library of Congress Cataloging-in-Publication Data

Ley, Graham.
A short introduction to the ancient Greek theater / Graham Ley. — Rev. ed.
   p.   cm.
Includes bibliographical references and index.
ISBN 0-226-47762-2 (cloth : alk. paper) — ISBN 0-226-47761-4 (pbk. : alk. paper)
1. Theater—Greece—History—To 500. 2. Greek drama—History and
criticism. I. Title. II. Title: Ancient Greek theater.

PA3201.L47   2006
792.0938—dc22

                                                    2006007437

CONTENTS

List of Plans and Illustrations vii
Preface ix
Preface to the Revised Edition x
Acknowledgments xi

Introduction 1
Greek Drama 5
The Organization of the Festivals 7
Lesser Dramatic Performances at Athens 10
The Writer 14
The Theater 17
Scenography 23
Masks, Costume, and Properties 25
Chorus 30
Actors 34
Reading Texts as Scripts 39
The Playing Space 44
The Audience 49
Delivery 54
Distance and Physical Action 60
Choral Song and Choral Action 65

Parody 74
Translation and Adaptation 82

Appendix: Chronology of the Surviving Plays 93
Glossary 95
Bibliography 97
Commentary on the Plates 117
General Index 121
Index of Plays 125

LIST *of* PLANS
& ILLUSTRATIONS

Plans

1   Relative location of theater, assembly, and *agora* in Athens 3
2a The early *orchestra* 18
2b Side view (same) 18
3a Schematic diagram of the developed fifth-century theater at Athens 19
3b Side view of theater 19
4a Diagram of the political assembly 51
4b Elevation of the political assembly 51

Plates

following page 108

1   Performer and chorus
2   Performers dressing
3   Prometheus and satyrs
4   *Aulos* player flanked by performers dressed as cocks
5   Illustration of Euripides' *Andromeda*
6   Illustration of Euripides' *Antiope*
7   Female acrobat with comic performer

PREFACE

I should like to express my thanks to all those who have helped in the formation of this volume. Students from the Universities of London and Auckland are foremost in the list, but I should like to include Michael Ewans, Meg and Marcus Wilson, Philip Hardie, Stig Rudberg, John Penwill, Tony Boyle, and Teresa Rodrigues, and to thank Richard Mazillius for drawing the diagrams. Richard Hamilton of Bryn Mawr provided many acute comments in his reading for the University of Chicago Press, and I am extremely grateful for his time and attention. Firm acknowledgment is also due to the associate director of the Press, Penelope Kaiserlian, for her careful guidance through to publication, and perhaps especially to David Grene, coeditor of *The Complete Greek Tragedies,* for his advice and support throughout. The edited text has benefited from the amendments suggested by Jo Ann Kiser for the Press; any flaws that remain are my own. I should like to dedicate the book to my family.

Author's Note: Those exact line references I have given are to the Greek of the Oxford Classical Text of Aeschylus, Sophocles, Euripides, and Aristophanes. Most modern translations provide some indications of line numbers, but unfortunately these vary considerably in their frequency.

Preface to the Revised Edition

This revised edition incorporates a number of minor changes to the text, with a significant updating of the final bibliography. I should like to thank Maggie Hivnor at the Press for her encouragement, and Tony Williams, who drew a new set of diagrams.

ACKNOWLEDGMENTS

I am grateful to David Rudkin and Margaret Ramsay Ltd. for permission to quote from the Foreword to David Rudkin's version of Euripides' *Hippolytus,* published by Heinemann Educational Books in 1980. The translation of the choral song from Euripides' *Hippolytus* is from the version of that play by David Grene in *The Complete Greek Tragedies,* published by the University of Chicago Press, and I should like to thank David Grene and the Press for allowing its inclusion.

The illustrations are reproduced by kind permission from Antikenmuseum Basel und Sammlung Ludwig (plate 1); H. L. Pierce Fund, courtesy Museum of Fine Arts, Boston (plate 2); Ashmolean Museum, Oxford (plate 3); J. Paul Getty Museum, Malibu (plate 4); Staatliche Museen zu Berlin, Antikensammlung (plate 5); Antikenmuseum Berlin, Staatliche Museen, preussischer Kulturbesitz (plate 6); Ashmolean Museum, Oxford (plate 7). My thanks are due to the staff in the photographic and publications departments of all these museums for their help.

The short comment by J. P. Sartre on adaptation is from the introduction to his adaptation of Euripides' *Trojan Women,* English version by Ronald Duncan, published by Hamish Hamilton in 1967. The selection of short extracts from versions of Aeschylus' *Agamemnon* is taken, in the order of their presentation in the text below, from: Robert Potter's eighteenth-century translation; *The Agamemnon,* translated into English rhyming verse by Gilbert Murray, London, George Allen and Unwin, 1920; *The Agamemnon of Aeschylus,* translated by Louis MacNeice, London, Faber and Faber, 1936; *The Complete Greek Tragedies,* edited by David Grene and Richmond Lattimore, *Aeschylus 1, Oresteia,* translated with an introduction by Richmond Lattimore, Chicago, the University of Chicago Press, 1953; *Agamemnon,* edited with a commentary by Eduard Fraenkel, *Volume 1,* Prolegomena. Text. Translation, Oxford, Oxford University Press, 1950; Robert Lowell, *The Oresteia of Aeschylus,* New York, Farrar, Strauss, Giroux, 1978; *The Oresteia,* translated by Robert Fagles, Harmondsworth, Penguin Books, 1977; Tony Harrison, *Dramatic Verse 1973–1985,* Newcastle upon Tyne, Bloodaxe Books, 1985; Michael Ewans, *Aeschylus: The Oresteia,* Everyman, London and Vermont, Dent and Tuttle, 1995.

A SHORT INTRODUCTION *to*
the ANCIENT GREEK THEATER

INTRODUCTION

The texts of ancient Greek tragedy and comedy have survived for over two thousand years, because small numbers
of people thought they were worth preserving. Most modern
readers meet them in translation, and the readership for these
translations is perhaps a larger one than the plays have had at any
other stage in their life. So it seems right that, for the reader of
what was originally a performed work, some attempt should be
made to indicate the original performance conditions.

Readers in translation are obviously dependent on those who
have learned the ancient language; and it is fair to say that knowledge of the original language is at least a safeguard, if not essential, for the task of reconstruction that faces the professional
historian of theater. But probably more significant than that is a
wide reading of the plays, preferably over a number of years.

The main reason for this, perhaps ironically, is that the plays
themselves actually provide the most detailed body of evidence
on the theatrical conditions for which they were designed. I mention irony because for many of the original audience nothing
could have seemed more self-evident than the shape of the playing space, the color and design of the costumes, and the styles of
performance presented to them.

The position for us, of course, is completely reversed. With the exceptions of archaeological evidence, some vase painting, and occasional comment or anecdote, the material form of ancient theater is substantially lost. What is left is a task of reconstruction, largely based on deduction from the "scripts" that survive, with alternatives weighed, and one chosen. There can be no guarantee that any reconstruction will finally be accurate; but it should be consistent, and provide at least a coherent vision of what for the original audience must have been one particular arrangement at any one time.

The reason we can speak with some confidence of "one particular arrangement" is that most of the ancient Greek texts we have, with possibly one or two exceptions, were written for first performance in one place, and in one theater. The writers of the surviving ancient Greek tragedies and comedies were all Athenians; and the dramatic festivals for which they composed, in a period that stretches effectively from 475 to 400 B.C., took place in the theater dedicated to the god Dionysus, located in the sanctuary that contained his temple, on the southern slope of the *akropolis,* the citadel of Athens (fig. 1). In general it is clear from the surviving plays—to some of which specific dates are attached—that the conditions of performance varied very little over this period, as might be expected when a single theater is the prime location for all major theatrical activity.

I have tried to concentrate in this short book largely on questions affecting presentation, and on what we might term the "theatrical apparatus": the material resources of theater that any prospective writer aims to deploy. There are many other books of many different kinds on the Greek theater, and on Greek drama, and the reader is advised to consult those in answer to any question which this one fails to satisfy. As some help in this respect I have appended a short bibliography of works in English which might be next in line for someone with strong interests in this area.

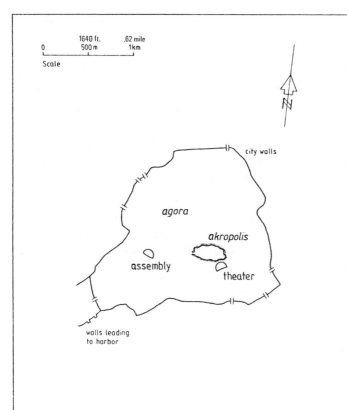

Scale

1640 ft.   .62 mile
0   500 m   1km

city walls

agora

akropolis

assembly

theater

walls leading
to harbor

fig.1   relative location of theater, assembly
and *agora* in Athens

For visual illustration, I have included a number of photographs of vase paintings from the period, and several schematic diagrams to provide some indication of the nature of the performance space and its place in the city of Athens. References are made to further illustrations from works cited in the concluding bibliography. (The titles in the references are abbreviated. See the bibliography for list of abbreviations.) The forms of the names of the tragic playwrights, and of their plays and the characters in them, are those used in *The Complete Greek Tragedies,* published by the University of Chicago Press. Some other names are given their familiar spellings. Less familiar Greek names, and the terms collected in the glossary at the back of this book, are transliterated (using "ch" in place of "kh": so *choros,* not *khoros*).

One final note: I have not attempted to include Menander, an Athenian comic writer who composed approximately in the years 320–290 B.C., because of the length of time that separates him from the period embracing the work of the other playwrights, and because a study of his theatrical practice for that reason needs to be made independently. So this work concentrates on what is known as the fifth century, 500–400 B.C., and plays presented at that time in the theater of Dionysus at Athens.

GREEK DRAMA

Greek drama, as usually described, includes the surviving tragedies (and satyr plays) of Aeschylus (c. 525–456 B.C.), Sophocles (c. 496–406 B.C.), and Euripides (c. 485–406 B.C.), and the comedies of Aristophanes (c. 450–385 B.C.) and Menander (c. 342–290 B.C.). Of these writers, Aeschylus is clearly the earliest, Sophocles and Euripides are near contemporaries, and Aristophanes is the youngest in the fifth century, though his writing career overlaps those of Sophocles and Euripides. Menander belongs to the end of the following century, and wrote comedies of a noticeably different kind from those of Aristophanes.

Since these plays are the primary source of interest in the Greek theater, as well as the most substantial evidence for its nature, some further details are necessary.

There are three kinds of play mentioned above. Of these, tragedy was considered predominantly serious and comedy was humorous. Satyr plays were composed by the tragedians, and were a grotesque relief from tragedy. It seems to be the case that no tragic writer wrote comedies, or comic writer tragedies.

Tragedy took its subject matter largely from the *muthoi* (myths or stories) which were expressed in the older narrative epic poems, of which only two, the *Iliad* and the *Odyssey* ascribed to Homer, survive. Comedy, in the hands of Aristophanes, was usually a contemporary fantasy, and was intended to be directly funny, as well as crude. The satyr play takes its name from the curious half-human, half-bestial creatures who were inevitable participants in the action, and who were called satyrs (plate 3). It has nothing to do with the later Roman form of poetry called "satire."

It is useful to speak of "surviving" plays because each writer, comic or tragic, composed far more than the number passed down from antiquity to the modern period. In the case of the later writer Menander, whose work was extremely popular in Egypt under its Greek and Roman administrations, excavations and careful methods of examining archaeological finds have revealed large fragments of his comedies. For the earlier dramatists, a modern reader is still mostly dependent on those few scripts that were copied in manuscript and preserved until the art of printing made them more widely available. A list of these surviving plays is given at the back of this book, with an approximate chronology. The gaps are very large: Aeschylus composed about eighty plays, Sophocles about one hundred and twenty, Euripides perhaps about ninety, and Aristophanes at least forty. In addition to these writers there were many more—some known by name—whose works are mostly lost, though some fragments remain, as do some fragments from the major playwrights.

THE ORGANIZATION
of the FESTIVALS

The festivals of Dionysus at Athens which included dramatic performances were known as the City, or Great, Dionysia and the Lenaea. The first of these was instituted before the beginning of the fifth century; dramatic performances at the Lenaea were officially recognized much later, just before 440 B.C. The City Dionysia remained by far the more important of the two dramatic festivals, though a comic writer such as Aristophanes seems to have written quite readily for both. The Lenaea took place in January, and the City Dionysia in late March/April. The likelihood is that almost all the surviving plays, both comedies and tragedies, were originally composed for performance in the theater of Dionysus, though there may be one or two exceptions.

The god Dionysus was one of the Olympian deities honored at Athens and widely elsewhere in the Greek world. In origin an ecstatic god, he was celebrated in a song known as the dithyramb, and his followers in myth were satyrs, lecherous and drunken, and *mainades,* the "mad women" of his rites. The association of drama with his festivals seems to be connected with an emphasis on song and dance in his worship, as well as on the mask. The City Dionysia was probably developed well before the end of the preceding century, but the details as we have them are of its organization under the democracy.

A tragic writer normally wrote three tragedies and one satyr play for one presentation at the City Dionysia. If the tragedies were connected in theme, then the presentation of those three plays is now known as a trilogy. Comic writers presented only one play at a time, though they might, it seems, write for both festivals in the same year. Performances at the Lenaea and the City Dionysia were competitions in honor of the patron god. At the City Dionysia each year three tragic writers competed against each other, and either three or five comic writers. There was no competition between comedies and tragedies. The audience must have watched four or five plays a day, for three or four days.

Apart from the major city festivals, there were also local celebrations in honor of Dionysus, held usually in the middle of winter in the townships of Attica, the region of which Athens was the capital city. There is clear evidence for the performance of plays at a number of these country Dionysia in the fourth century, and it is quite possible that some of these productions originated in the fifth century, certainly in locations like the Piraeus, the port of Athens. Whether the plays on these occasions were new, or revivals of popular tragedies and comedies seen at the major festivals, is not altogether clear. But later evidence suggests revivals, and the writers whose work survives seem to have concentrated on presenting new plays at the city festivals, notably the City Dionysia.

The official primarily responsible for the organization of the City Dionysia was the *archon,* a magistrate chosen annually by lot, and by whose name the year was known. It was to this magistrate, who assumed office in midsummer, that prospective playwrights "applied for a chorus," namely for official acceptance as one of the three tragedians, or three or five comic writers, whose works were to be performed in the following spring.

By what criterion the decision was made is unknown, nor is it clear how the playwrights presented their case to the magistrate.

The further organization of tragic, satyric, and comic production, and the bulk of the expense, then devolved on wealthy private citizens, selected as *choregoi,* or producers, for each playwright. The state paid for the actors, and the *choregos* paid for the training and costume of the chorus. There would appear to be a gap of about six months or more between the selection of a playwright and the performance of his work, and by at least the end of the fifth century there was a public announcement of the subjects of the plays, the *proagon,* shortly before the period of performance.

The introduction of a public subsidy for poorer citizens to attend the performances is attributed to the Athenian politician Pericles (d. 429 B.C.), and it is likely that tickets would have been in use from this period forward in the fifth century.

LESSER DRAMATIC
PERFORMANCES
at ATHENS

The evidence for forms of drama at Athens other than those supported by the state at the festivals of Dionysus is extremely interesting, but yields only the haziest of pictures. Both Plato and Xenophon refer to puppets, and although they are writing in the fourth century it is most unlikely that puppetry was an innovation of their own era. From these and other references in later antiquity it is clear that some form of articulated puppets, which may have had a resemblance to larger automata, or apparently self-moving figures, were in use, and the Greek term *neurospastos* ("drawn/operated by cord") suggests marionettes. The figures, however, may have been operated by internal, hidden cords. When Plato refers in his *Republic* to the display of puppets above a screen, which in his description is like a low wall, it is tempting from the comparative context of our knowledge of puppetry to interpret this as referring to hand or glove puppets rather than articulated figures. There is no good reason to rule out the parallel existence of both forms.

What this puppet theater was like, and where and for whom

it was performed, are difficult questions to answer, but some of the accounts do give an impression. Plato compares the strings to emotions that pull us about, moving us back and forth in contrasting actions. Plato is making a comparison, deploying the metaphor of the human being as a puppet to which we owe many of the references, but it may well be that he is alluding to a lively performance. Contrasting emotions are familiar from Greek drama, and as one of its resources manipulation permits a vigorous rather than a restrained convention. Plato also offers us in his dialogue *Laws* one certainty about the composition of the audience, since he concludes without hesitation that the youngest children would approve of puppetry, while older children would approve of comedy. One late author from the Roman period does refer to a puppeteer performing in the theater that was home to the tragedies of Euripides, but this reference implies a contrast between different eras, although we cannot be certain that puppets did not appear in the theaters of Athens and the townships of Attica outside the regulated times of the festivals.

Our speculations about the subject matter must rest between the mythical and heroic, or the everyday, and it may be relevant that comedy seems to have used both of these divergent sources of inspiration for its plots. Whether puppet performances at Athens were ever substantially serious—as with many cultures, but in contrast to Plato's apparent association of puppetry with comedy—cannot be known. Comedy would certainly have provided a model of physical knockabout, but like comedy the puppet theater might have drawn on a ready source of parody in tragic plots and performance. Perhaps the most obvious candidate for a puppet character, in our heavily restricted view, must be a folk hero such as Heracles, with his club, his appetites, and his bravado. Puppetry is also a theater of sounds, as well as actions and voices; it would be very surprising if farting was not involved.

The dramatic form known as mime flourished in Sicily, and the earliest composer of scripts for it known to us is Sophron, from the Greek city of Syracuse, who was a contemporary of Sophocles and Euripides. This early mime was quite unlike modern mime, since it used speech, and the limited evidence from the fragments of Sophron's compositions shows scripts written in prose, which were later classified into men's and women's mimes. The classification is textual, and seems to refer to the gender of the leading characters, suggesting that Sophron exploited situations that caricatured both genders in relative isolation from each other. Whether that distinction extended to the performers is a tantalizing question; comparative evidence from the Greek theater would suggest it did not. The performers may have used masks, as well as costumes and some properties. As far as the titles and fragments of Sophron reveal, the situations were domestic, with the scripts involving sex and food, obscene connections between them, and attempts to use rituals to gain a desired end. Extended solo speech punctuated by instructions or asides to others attending may have been varied by dialogue, and plainly a small ensemble was often required.

Sophron's mimes may have been intended for private performance, and it is clear that at some point during the fourth century at least the scripts came to Athens as texts. But there is good evidence that some Sicilian ensembles came in person much earlier than that, to exploit a ready and lucrative market. A dialogue by Xenophon, *Symposium,* set in the later part of the fifth century and written relatively early in the fourth century, reveals the entertainment that Xenophon thought his readership would accept as occurring in the house of a wealthy Athenian at a men's dinner party, the symposium of the title. This is provided by a small ensemble of slaves, owned by a Syracusan, composed of a young female slave playing the pipes, a slave boy who sings and plays the lyre, and a young female dancer and acrobat (plate 7).

At the close of the dialogue and the symposium, a performance is presented of the union of Dionysus with Ariadne, which incorporates dancing by the boy playing Dionysus, and some dialogue between him and the young female acrobat as Ariadne, to music from the piper. It has been directed by the Syracusan, and culminates in what is described as an explicit, physical enactment of kissing and sexual foreplay.

This is an unmasked performance, and the account of it is itself fictional, but it provides a fascinating glimpse into private entertainments at Athens. The Syracusan is made to remark that he has a lucrative business, and in passing he says he is grateful to fools for watching his puppets; the word used is *neurospasta,* that we might translate as marionettes. It seems most logical to take this as a metaphorical reference to the ensemble under his control, but it confirms the familiarity of puppets to Xenophon's readership. The young female performer in this piece, and the differences this mini-drama shows from what we can detect about the mimes scripted by Sophron, suggest that the variety of dramatic performances in the late fifth century at Athens may have been much greater than we can know.

THE WRITER

The official term for the playwright in the festival records is *didaskalos,* which means "teacher" or "trainer," and this title refers to an original function as trainer of the chorus, a group of dancing singers who formed the core of dramatic performance. But later, with the introduction of solo actors, the term will probably have been understood to cover the preparation of a fixed script and musical form for production. It seems that the playwright was also regularly responsible for what we would now call theatrical direction, as well as for the composition of spoken and sung text. But the comic writer Aristophanes handed over some of his plays to other directors, and scattered evidence suggests this practice may not have been uncommon for comedy in the later fifth century. The degree to which an enthusiastic and committed *choregos,* by taking care of much of the expense of the production, might intrude upon direction is unclear; but it would seem that his principal responsibility was for the fitness, skills, and presentation of the chorus.

All plays were composed in verse. The spoken verse, largely for the actors, was usually in the iambic meter, considered close to the rhythms of normal speech. Songs for the chorus, and occasionally for actors, were in a variety of meters and modes. One essential for the playwright would almost certainly be an advanced training in the art of (choral) song composition, and probably in dance. All the dramatic writers whom we know seem to have started composing plays as young men, which suggests that the activity followed closely on education, which will have involved some attention to the work of prominent past poets and songwriters.

Choice of form may have been easy, because it was definite. For the intending tragic writer, there was a brief period in the earlier fifth century when it was possible to compose on events taken from recent military struggles. This was apparently succeeded by an almost constant expectation that subjects for tragedies would be taken from the lives and actions of mythical figures, as these were represented by the poems that existed about them, or by the spoken traditions or rituals associated with them and with various localities. These sources—when combined with the curious cowardice and licentiousness that characterized the unvarying chorus of satyrs—would also provide much of the substance for the composition of satyr plays.

For the comic writer, there is the evidence of Aristophanes, who would seem to be as attracted to the opportunity to make his audience laugh at the fantastic aspirations of his characters as he is to the chance to be amusingly provocative on issues of contemporary concern. A similar, if not the same, capacity for the composition of spoken verse and song as in tragedy and a fascination with the techniques of theatrical humor would provide the backbone of the art. For later comedy, in the work of Menander, there is evidence for a greater ethical interest in the actions and motives of comic characters, which may reflect the influence of contemporary philosophy. Both comic writers show a profound interest in tragedy.

Although successful playwrights were granted a prize, it is not known what this amounted to, nor is it likely that the existence of a prize encouraged the development of a class of playwrights who supported themselves by composition. The evidence is to the contrary, and the writers whose work survives appear to have belonged to the wide category of Athenians whose landholding was large enough to support them, and to provide them with the leisure to involve themselves in public life.

Biographical details on the writers are not substantial, and where they do exist it is not clear how much reliance should be placed on them. But tradition records that Sophocles was prominent in music and dance from an early age, and that he originally performed as an actor in his own early plays. His later role in public life included service as a general, and as treasurer for the Athenian military alliance. His respect for organized religion is also recorded, as are the statements that he wrote a work on the chorus (now lost) and founded a religious association in honor of the Muses. His son, Iophon, became a playwright, and Sophocles himself is said never to have been placed third in a dramatic competition. It is a reasonably convincing picture, and may well be accurate.

THE THEATER

The location for the City festival of Dionysus was the theater in the precinct of the god on the south slope of the citadel of Athens, the *akropolis*. Many changes were made to the theater in antiquity, and the present ruins largely reflect the foundations and first levels of a version of the theater constructed far later than the fifth century B.C.

Archaeology considers layers, and investigations of the ruins of the theater of Dionysus, along with comparisons with other Greek theaters, have established some reasonable conclusions about the nature of the original playing space and its development.

The earliest evidence for performances in the precinct seems to be for a circular dancing space, an *orchestra,* on a flattened terrace at the foot of the hill, and associated with a small temple of Dionysus (figs. 2a and 2b). This suggests the presence of choral songs and dances. The choice of the slope of the *akropolis* for the *orchestra,* and perhaps in principle for the precinct of Dionysus, may well have been dependent on the ease with which a hillside can accommodate an audience. This would then provide a natural *theatron,* or "watching-place." Other evidence suggests, contrastingly, that some early performances may have taken place in the *agora,* on ground set aside in the city for trade and cult (fig. 1), and in which there was still an area known as the *orchestra*

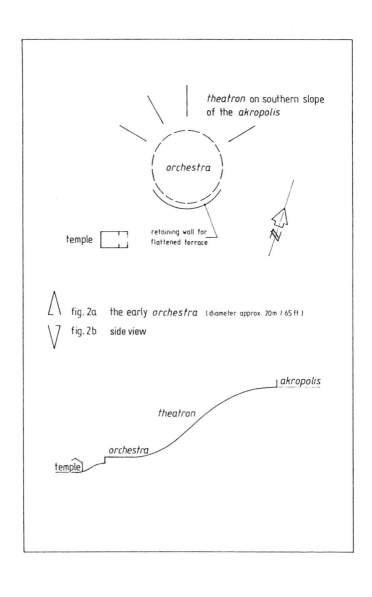

theatron on southern slope
of the *akropolis*

orchestra

retaining wall for
flattened terrace

temple

fig. 2a   the early *orchestra* (diameter approx. 20m / 65 ft)

fig. 2b   side view

akropolis

theatron

orchestra

temple

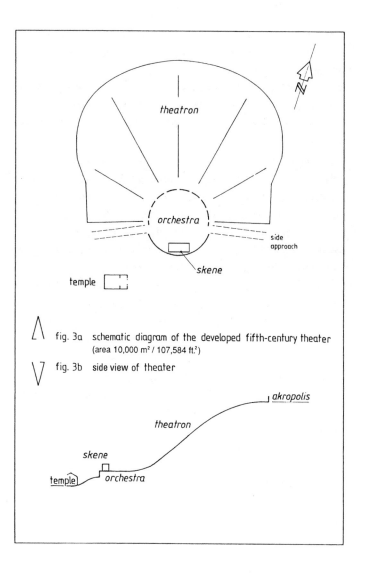

theatron

orchestra

side
approach

skene

temple

fig. 3a   schematic diagram of the developed fifth-century theater
(area 10,000 m² / 107,584 ft.²)

fig. 3b   side view of theater

akropolis

theatron

skene

temple   orchestra

at the end of the fifth century. But by the time of the earliest surviving plays there can be little doubt that dramatic performances took place in the theater.

The developed shape of the theater (the term comes to be applied to the whole) includes three components (figs. 3a and 3b): an extensive *theatron,* with the hill hollowed out and stepped, perhaps mostly with boards, but later consolidated in stone, accommodating eventually up to fourteen thousand spectators; an *orchestra,* probably circular in the fifth century, in which a chorus could sing and dance; and, additionally, the *skene* or scene building, which included a door. Of these three components, the *skene* poses the most problems, because the foundations provide no precise evidence for its elevation, and there are no certain illustrations of a *skene* dating from the fifth century.

The earliest surviving plays—the earlier tragedies of Aeschylus—seem to have been performed without a scene building. But the surviving trilogy known as the *Oresteia,* produced in 458 B.C., initiates a period, which then lasts as long as the convention itself, in which a scene building of some sort is clearly involved in the performance both of tragedies and comedies.

The word *skene* simply means tent, and presumably this reflects a time when a tent or booth (perhaps with a wooden frame) was used. But in the first play of the *Oresteia* a character appears on the roof, and in the second play there is a practicable door, while in the earlier plays of Aeschylus it is difficult to find any suggestion that a tent was deployed as a substantial indication of setting, though the actors certainly did have to change masks and costume during their performance. Perhaps a *skene* was used for this purpose.

The initial construction of a solid *skene* would almost certainly have been from wood. From the beginning there are clear signs that it contained the machinery later known as an *ekkuk-*

lema, used in tragedy for the display of corpses. This appears to have been a mobile platform that could be projected from the doors that are logically assumed to have been centrally placed in the *skene.* By the time of the production of the *Oresteia,* and of the known construction of the *skene,* the Athenians had considerable experience in the traction of heavy wooden objects, as a result of the construction and renovation of their many fighting ships (triremes). The details of the machinery remain unknown, but the principles of its operation are relatively clear.

An additional machine was added to the scene building later in the fifth century, certainly before 431 B.C., with the production of Euripides' *Medea,* and perhaps not long before. This was the *mechane,* or crane, which could lift actors and suspend them above or in front of the *skene.* That the *mechane* was used for striking visual effect is clear from its involvement in plays where an animal (Pegasus, the flying horse of Bellerophon) or an object (the chariot of the sun, used by Medea) adds substance to the illusion.

It seems most likely that the *skene* was originally placed inside and to the rear of the *orchestra* terrace itself (figs. 3a and 3b). But the nature and chronology of its development from that time forward are obscure. Stone foundations for the scene building are variously dated to the later part of the fifth century, or to a period just after 400 B.C. or even later. The most likely assumption—and it should be no more—is that alterations to the retaining wall of the *theatron,* known to be made in the time of Pericles in connection with the construction of the neighboring Odeum, should be associated with developments toward permanence in the *skene,* which could then accommodate the *mechane.* Further stages in adaptation and construction finally resulted in both *theatron* and *skene* being fully established in expensive stone by the later part of the fourth century.

The major problems concerning the construction and form

of the *skene* are accompanied by some doubts over the shape of the *orchestra,* of which the regular circle familiar from pictures of the later theater at Epidaurus may prove to be an inaccurate representation. So the diagrams presented here must be taken to be no more than provisional, in sketching the relation of parts to the whole.

SCENOGRAPHY

S*kenographia,* literally "painting of/on a *skene,*" with an associated term *skiagraphia,* which refers to the "painting of shadows," are the words used to describe what on occasions has been doubted, namely the indication of theatrical setting by painting, most probably on panels. This innovation is ascribed either to Aeschylus or to Sophocles in the sources, and these indications, if reliable, would place it in the same immediate period as the introduction of the third actor ("Actors," below) and the construction of the *skene.*

Major narrative painting in Athens and elsewhere in Greece was displayed on the interior walls of public buildings, and seems to date as a distinct development from the period of the earliest surviving plays. This is clearly interesting in relation to the construction of the *skene,* because the later foundations provide evidence for a facade, in a series of postholes on either side of what must be a foundation for a central door, and a facade could easily be used to display a series of painted panels indicating setting.

The Roman writer Vitruvius states in his treatise on architecture that the painter Agatharchos, who worked for Aeschylus and left a commentary on his creation, influenced other near-contemporaries to write on the use of perspective in scene painting. Vitruvius explicitly refers to the use of perspective in the representation of buildings, and temples and grander private houses, or "palaces," were certainly two of the most regular settings for tragedy. It would not be difficult to match this consistency in "background" with Vitruvius' statement, and with a growing interest in a limited form of perspective, stimulated by the opportunity to decorate and define the theatrical *skene.*

Further evidence concerns the satyr plays, which would appear to have made repeated use of a cave for their settings. This same, or a similar, location appears also in surviving tragedy (Sophocles' *Philoctetes*) and in comedy (Aristophanes' *Birds*), and evidence from vase painting (plates 5 and 6, Euripides' lost tragedies *Andromeda* and *Antiope*) confirms that rocks, trees, and shrubs were associated with representations of the cave in tragedy.

A striking change of setting in one tragedy (Sophocles' *Ajax,* from military tent to deserted shoreline), and the contrasting locations of plays linked in one presentation (Euripides' *Helen,* set in front of a palace, and his lost *Andromeda,* set on the seacoast in front of a cave) might best be explained by reference to the resources of painting on panels. The limited range for visual representation would then contain the temple, the palace or larger private house, the cave or other natural setting, and an occasional ironic variation, such as the farmer's hut in Euripides' *Electra.*

It cannot be at all clear, from the nature of the available evidence, whether *skenographia* was considered by later theorists to have been used for comic performance in this period. But the surviving scripts can certainly remove performers and a diversity of properties abruptly ("The Playing Space" and "Distance and Physical Action" below), and abruptness in the change of setting in some surviving plays might reflect the same unrecorded activity in support of presentation. If the satyr play made use of a cave, then *skenographia* should not be excluded as a possibility for a form of performance as strongly visual as fifth-century comedy.

MASKS, COSTUME,

& PROPERTIES

M asks (*prosopa*) and decorated costume are known to have been significant elements of the worship of the god Dionysus at Athens, and it is at least likely that their use in rites and celebration predates the emergence of drama. Specifically, vase paintings in nondramatic contexts show a mask of the god suspended from a tree with a decorated robe hanging below it to form an icon of the deity, around which dancers may be gathered. The existence of these material elements would allow, with little immediate innovation, for the presentation of early drama.

Illustrations of theatrical masks on Athenian vases from the fifth century reveal a full head mask, with no particular distortion, for tragic performance: of a kind that appears to take its dimensions from the contradictory demands of close assimilation to the distance between the performers' eyes and mouth (laterally and vertically) and the need to envelop the head (*DFA*, figs. 32 and 33). The result is, almost inevitably, an exaggerated jaw. Chorus members for tragedy were masked and costumed in a very similar manner to actors, as more than one vase from the period shows (plate 2). The materials used were fragile, and almost certainly light: linen and wood are possible components, and some form of paste (plaster, mortar) seems a far more plausible candidate for the shaping and stiffening of the facial areas than the only likely alternative, wax. Masks may have been stored, but the differentiation needed in the range of roles or the requirements of actors will have meant that the mask makers, the *prosopopoioi,* will have been fairly active. For the City Dionysia in one year alone, fifteen to seventeen plays with an average of twenty and more performers add up to a formidable total.

More can be said about masks than is probably appropriate here. Some of the major points are these:

FOR COMEDY, there is strong evidence that some masks were modeled directly on life, to provide a caricature of a known individual. Some politicians, playwrights, and other figures, notably the philosopher Socrates, were perhaps portrayed in this way.

COMIC MASKS were distortions, but unfortunately almost all the visual evidence applies to periods later than the fifth century (but see plate 4). A rigid categorization by type, and perhaps by masks in an extended but fixed series (e.g., the running slave, the old man, the young girl, etc.), is almost certainly a later development, though it may well have its roots in Aristophanic comedy.

THE SCRIPTS on a number of occasions reveal some characteristics of a particular mask. One of the best examples is the picture that emerges of the mask of the god Dionysus when he is apprehended and questioned by Pentheus in Euripides' tragedy *The Bacchae.*

THE USE of masks lent itself to specific effects. Not only did it mean that an individual actor might appear and reappear as several different characters, but a powerful effect might be achieved by altering or changing the mask for the same character within a play. In Euripides' *Helen,* Helen enters the scene building to reappear with a change of

costume and an altered mask, in pretended mourning; and in Sophocles' *Oedipus the King* and Euripides' *Hecuba,* both Oedipus and Poly-
mestor enter the scene building toward the climax of the plays to reappear blinded.

EURIPIDES MAY well have made use of the same mask for Helen in
his *Trojan Women* in 415 B.C. as for his radically different presentation
of Helen in the play of that name dated securely at 412 B.C. Other possibilities of reuse may also be found from the same period, in Euripides' surviving tragedies.

The costume for tragedy was, it appears, always decorative,
though it seems to have been based largely on a selective presentation of familiar, contemporary garments. There is some evidence, from vase paintings, that theatrical costume became more
elaborate during the course of the century (compare plates 1 and
2 with plate 5), and further evidence confirms that oriental or
non-Greek costume was distinctive (*IGD* III.2.1). Fabric might
also be used as a substantial property, as it is in the reception of
Agamemnon into the scene building in the *Oresteia* of Aeschylus.
The weaving or dyeing of elaborate garments is attested for various forms of cult, and the adaptation of this attention to theatrical performance cannot have posed many serious problems.
At least in tragedy performers might be given soft calf-length
boots, perhaps known as *kothornoi,* with a curved toe and slipper
base suitable for swift movement (plate 2).

Costume is of crucial importance in determining characters
or chorus by status, sex, provenance, or condition of life. In his
comedy *Frogs,* Aristophanes suggests that Aeschylus had used
more solemn costume than the rags favored by Euripides. But in
the earliest surviving play of Aeschylus, *The Persians,* the defeated
Persian king Xerxes returns in tatters; while in Euripides' *Andromache* and *Trojan Women* Hermione and Helen appear in finery,

in explicit contrast to women who are slaves. Slaves, refugees, non-Greeks, warriors, powerful men and women, gods, and the servants of gods all make their appearance in the surviving tragedies of Aeschylus, and there is little to suggest that this range was narrowed over the course of the century. Some varieties of garment may be illustrated accurately on the available vases; but again it is Euripides' *Bacchae,* with its ironic delight in dressing the rigid authoritarian ruler Pentheus in the clothing of a woman worshipper of Dionysus, which provides the most exact and detailed description of any one costume in the surviving tragedies.

For comedy, there is occasional evidence that the actors might wear a hugely exaggerated penis, as part of a traditional costume dependent on the close association of the male member (*phallos*) with the worship of the god Dionysus (plate 4). Otherwise, costume design might vary wildly, and fantastically, with the concept of the play: in Aristophanes' *Birds* there are clear indications that each chorus member represented a different wild bird, and the predominance of animal choruses in fifth-century comedy (*Wasps, Frogs*) and of inanimate objects (*Clouds* and *Transport Ships,* the latter a lost play) suggests visual ingenuity on an elaborate scale. An immense variety of comic costume, combined in spectacle, is also apparent from the opening scene of Aristophanes' *Acharnians.*

For the satyr play, we have the benefit of a representation of a complete cast on what seems to be a celebration vase, from about the end of the century (*DFA,* fig. 49; *HGRT,* fig. 20). From this painting, and from others, it is clear that the satyr mask was snubnosed, and that a loincloth of linen or of goatskin was worn, with an erect but not exaggerated penis and a horsetail. The leader of the satyrs was known as Silenus, who would seem to have been characterized by a more complete body stocking covered in white fur, and portrayed as old and white-haired.

Properties are abundant in comedy, with a particular emphasis on all the equipment of an *oikos,* or household, with repeated attention to kitchen implements. Contrived properties may form a spectacular opening to a play, such as the giant dung beetle attached to the *mechane* in Aristophanes' *Peace,* or a visual adjunct to what is already a preposterous scene, such as the doubtlessly enlarged and possibly human-powered cheese grater in the remarkable trial of the dog in *Wasps.*

In this last case, a property may come close to being a costume, and for tragedy a more restrained use of props could confirm any expectation received from myth, or from familiar illustration in painting or sculpture. It is inherently likely that both Apollo and Artemis will carry a bow, and, possibly, threaten to use it. So, for all three forms of play in which he could be made to appear, the expectation will be that Heracles should be clothed in a lion skin and be seen carrying a club, with perhaps his bow slung over his shoulders.

Properties may be a means of identification, but that also may lead to a wider significance. Philoctetes, in Sophocles' play, is the inheritor of Heracles' bow; but it is fundamentally the bow, if not the man himself, that Odysseus and Neoptolemus have come to take with them to Troy, and its presence and its handling divides and unites the characters repeatedly throughout the tragedy.

Aristophanes parodies Euripides' use of properties (as well as costume) in his comedy *Acharnians,* and their significance in setting the tone of a play is paralleled by their crucial action within a play. A casket conveys the deadly robe to the daughter of Creon in Euripides' *Medea,* and another carries a similarly deadly robe to Heracles in Sophocles' *Women of Trachis.* Orestes stands to one side in Sophocles' *Electra* while his sister laments over an empty urn, supposedly containing his ashes.

Properties are of the essence of Athenian theater, and their great advantage for a modern vision of performance is that we can rely very often on decisive references to them in the scripts.

CHORUS

The Greek word *choros* describes a group of people expected to sing and dance. The chorus for tragedy was apparently increased in number near the middle of the fifth century from twelve to fifteen; the chorus for comedy numbered twenty-four. There is no clear evidence for the size of the satyr chorus.

The history of the *choros* in Greek society is a long and complex one, and is bound up firmly with many varieties of Greek poetry, apart from drama. Most simply expressed, it is clear that songs or dances accompanied decisive events in the lives of Greek communities, and that eventually literacy, namely the record offered to us by the reintroduction of writing into Greece before 700 B.C., permits us to glimpse the organization of what originally may have been spontaneous or traditional forms into what we recognize as poetry. Those skilled in composition (verbal and musical) might be required or requested to provide a song for a particular event, such as a marriage, an athletic victory, the funeral of a member of a wealthy family, or a religious festival. This practice continued well into the fifth century and beyond, and many of the songs will have been sung by a chorus, often acting as representatives of a community.

A tragic *choros* in honor of the god Dionysus is first mentioned in connection with the sixth century, not at Athens; but convincing evidence for the widespread existence of *choroi* throughout the Greek world (in the western Greek settlements in Sicily and Italy, in Sparta, on the island of Delos in honor of the gods Apollo and Artemis) makes particular explanations for their presence at Athens unnecessary.

The use of the mask in Dionysiac worship may well have encouraged representation. The activities of *choroi* were in any case performances, and the need for a composer as trainer (*didaskalos*, the later "playwright") is hardly surprising. What does seem to be distinct is the step by which this figure—and, for Athens, the earliest name is Thespis—began to take a part in the performance, from which origins the concept of the actor, and the speaking parts, gradually arose.

If tragedy was in origin "a" choral song, one of many different kinds but characterized by its dedication to Dionysus, then the major difference between that and the form that confronts us as developed "drama" is constituted by the juxtaposition of spoken sections and song. The presence of the chorus in the surviving plays of Aeschylus is often substantial, with extensive sections of the play dependent on the continuity achieved through choral song and dance. In later tragedy the standard pattern is for this contribution to be made in a more distinctly intermittent way, as a series of independent "songs"—usually known as "odes," from the Greek word for song—which reveal a tendency toward the end of the century to discard their direct relevance to the action of the play.

For comedy, the situation is far more problematic, because the earliest surviving plays are very late (the earliest, Aristophanes' *Acharnians,* was produced in 425 B.C.), and because the origins and development of comedy as a theatrical form rapidly became obscure even in antiquity. One likely explanation sees the origin of comedy in a *komos,* a disorderly and irreverent procession in honor of the god Dionysus. The introduction of comedy into the

City festival at a later date than tragedy, in 486 B.C., and the number granted to its chorus (double that originally given to tragedy) might then suggest that comedy, in its theatrical form, was in part modeled on the precedent given by tragedy.

Certain aspects of the comic chorus as it is found in the plays of Aristophanes appear to be traditional elements, though how far back these traditions go is impossible to judge. Of these the most notable is what was known as the *parabasis:* at a relatively central moment of the drama the chorus "steps forward/aside," its members perhaps disencumbering themselves of any properties they may have, and addresses the audience directly in an apparently corrective manner and on behalf of the dramatist.

The recurrence of an animal chorus for comedy has been mentioned. Here again, tradition is evident, because vase paintings from the early fifth century and before show men dressed as birds; men as horses, with other men riding on their backs (*IGD* I.9, *DTC* pl. VII: Aristophanes' *Knights* suggests a comparison); and men riding on dolphins and ostriches (*DTC* pl. VIII.b), in what would seem to be representations of choruses. The degree of theatrical realization for any concept of a chorus must remain uncertain; but it was clearly ambitious, and titles such as *Clouds, Transport Ships,* and *Islands* would seem to confirm a reliance on something more than costume (as clothing) for the effect.

In later comedy, beginning in a tendency noticeable by the end of the fifth century and confirmed in the fourth, the role given to the chorus diminished rapidly. In the comedies of Menander there is no written script for choral song, merely a notation that a chorus performed at four points in the play, dividing what would now be called five acts. In Aristophanes' early comedies the chorus helps to define the play, often as a visual joke and by close involvement in the action of the play; by the time of Menander the chorus provides only a subsidiary entertainment, totally disjoined from the actors.

There is some reason to believe that the satyr play was introduced to maintain a strong Dionysiac element in dramatic production. Satyrs were closely associated with Dionysus, and the development of tragedy toward a wide range of mythical subjects may have prompted the introduction of a form that by convention, in the unchanging nature of its chorus, ensured a tribute to the god in whose name the festival was undertaken. The one complete text of a satyr play that survives, Euripides' *Cyclops*, taken with the visual evidence of the vase painting of the cast for a satyric production (*DFA*, fig. 49; *HGRT*, fig. 20), provides a relatively firm picture of the entertainment involved. The satyric chorus would be expected to dance and sing (plate 3), and might well be active in the course of the play.

The choice of a chorus for dramatic performances is known to have been the responsibility of the *choregos*, but there is no firm evidence for the methods of selection used during the fifth century.

ACTORS

The original actor in tragedy was the composer, and initially there was only one. The early plays of Aeschylus seem to require only two actors, and ancient sources state that Aeschylus was responsible for the introduction of the second performer. Aeschylus produced the *Oresteia* in 458 B.C., and for that trilogy three actors are required. Sources ascribe the introduction of the third actor either to Aeschylus or to Sophocles, who first won the tragic prize in 468 B.C. The confusion is easy to explain if the innovation came at some time during that decade, when Aeschylus and Sophocles were active together. In 449 B.C. a competition was begun for the leading actors of each of the year's three tragic presentations at the City Dionysia. Probably before this time the practice of composers performing in their own works had ended: Sophocles was the first to make this decision, and it may well have come alongside the introduction of the third actor.

The Greek word for actor was *hypokrites,* which probably meant "answerer" originally: the composer, in taking a part in performance, is extremely likely to have "answered" the chorus. The evidence suggests that from the beginning, the actor predominantly spoke, although some acted parts in the tragedies of Aeschylus also required singing and dancing. The actor will have spoken or chanted verse, which initially must have been delivered either to the chorus or directly to the audience. One tradition ascribes the invention of the spoken parts of tragedy to the first named composer, Thespis, and this seems perfectly plausible.

One actor, with the aid of a selection of masks and costumes and the resource of a *skene,* might take several roles. The original advantages of a second performer are not so easy to determine: the obvious thought, for those influenced by later forms of drama, is the possibility of dialogue between actors as characters, known in later Greek terminology as *stichomuthia.* But, in fact, the earlier plays of Aeschylus show relatively little use of dialogue between actors. The principal reason for this is the direct relationship that most characters have to the chorus, or—to express this more precisely—the emphasis placed in these early plays on the reaction of the chorus to any communication made to it by a character. A growing complexity in the diversity of roles, and the advantages of a greater flexibility in the introduction or removal of characters, seem ultimately the most likely explanations for the innovation. Simple strain on the voice and physique of the composer-performer as roles increased may also have been a factor.

For two-actor tragedy, the division of roles would be a relatively simple problem, and it is not really possible to detect any striking imbalance in demands made on either performer. This is perhaps because there are only three plays of Aeschylus which appear to demonstrate this early two-actor form—*The Persians* (472 B.C.), *Seven against Thebes* (467 B.C.) and *The Suppliant Maidens* (463 B.C.)—and these all come from separate productions.

In Aeschylus' *Oresteia* trilogy of 458 B.C.—a group of three surviving tragedies—three actors are required, with the possible momentary addition of a fourth in the second play, and the diversity of roles poses far greater problems for their attribution to individual actors. But the certain demands on all three performers are remarkably even, and the introduction and removal of characters throughout the trilogy could allow the same performer to play the same characters in successive plays, and the same actor to play both father and son, mother and daughter. The advantages of this system of association are obvious, in a form so heavily dependent on the voice, and it was perhaps employed.

In the other surviving tragedies, all of which may well belong to the period after the actors' competition was instituted in 449 B.C., it is important to notice the regular presence of a leading character, whose prominence in the action of a play would almost certainly have justified the attribution of that role to a leading actor, who was in competition with other leading actors. The need to gratify actors and audience with prominent roles may have dictated this emphasis. Otherwise, it would seem that the demands on tragic performers remained very much the same throughout the century, with the occasional requirement for extended singing and dancing, often in conjunction with the chorus.

The usual allocation of actors in tragedy was three, though *Alcestis* (438 B.C.) and *Medea* (431 B.C.) by Euripides might with some difficulty be acted by two, and there are some occasions when four seem to be needed (Aeschylus' *Libation Bearers* in his *Oresteia,* mentioned above, and Sophocles' *Oedipus at Colonus*). The limitation to three as a normal practice may be no more than pragmatic, and perhaps a result of the difficulties of identifying different speakers in a convention using full head masks. In addition, there may be nonspeaking masked characters, speaking or singing children, and almost any number of supernumeraries.

Conclusions about comic performance in the fifth century are largely limited to Aristophanes. Comedy seems able to use more than three masked actors, although an assumption of three would account for the substance of many of the surviving plays. The demands made on comic actors were inevitably very different from those made on tragic performers, and it is extremely unlikely that the same men would play in both forms. Aristophanic comedy is active, places a far more telling emphasis on dialogue and timing; and though it may throw one character into verbal prominence, many of its effects are achieved through physical routines involving two or more characters, or character(s) and chorus. The capacity for acknowledged audience address, an abusive familiarity, mimicry, and the ludicrous qualities of many solo songs again distance the demands of the form from the relative consistency of tragedy. There was no prize for comic acting at the City Dionysia until late in the fourth century, though there was at the Lenaea from about 440 B.C., where there was also a prize for tragic acting.

The names of a few actors are preserved from the fifth century, along with the information that the playwrights made regular use of particular performers. Aeschylus is said to have had firstly Kleandros and then in addition Mynniskos as his performers. Whether Aeschylus acted all his life is not clear: the demands posed by any of the leading roles in the *Oresteia* would seem to be formidable to a man in his sixties, but this may be a false impression. So there is just a possibility that we may know the names of the cast for the *Oresteia* in 458 B.C. (Aeschylus, Kleandros, Mynniskos).

In the written tradition, Sophocles is associated with an actor called Tlepolemos; but a series of pictures on vases suggested to the scholar T. B. L. Webster the association of another performer with productions by Sophocles. The name Euaion, son of Aeschylus, is placed next to that of Perseus on a vase illustrating Perseus arriving to rescue Andromeda (*IGD* III.2.1), and recurs on a second vase that can be directly linked to a tragedy (*Thamyras,* now lost) by Sophocles (*IGD* III.2.9). The likelihood is that Euaion was an actor, and since Sophocles wrote an *Andromeda,* as well as *Thamyras,* the association seems certain. Written tradition records that Sophocles himself acted the part of Thamyras, which required him to sing and play the lyre; and on the painting Euaion's name is placed next to that of an elderly woman, who is probably to be identified with Argiope, the mother of Thamyras. The play will have been relatively early, since later Sophocles stopped acting because of weakness in his voice.

All the actors, as well as all the chorus members, for all three forms of play, were men.

READING TEXTS
as SCRIPTS

L earning to read the surviving texts of Greek tragedy and comedy as scripts for performance is particularly important in the absence of any contemporary description of fifth-century production in the theater of Dionysus at Athens. This is the case whether our interest is in producing them ourselves, or in how they were originally produced. Even if the intention is to adapt a play, or to take its action as an inspiration for creating a new theater piece, taking the trouble to find out how a play works will yield far more than any casual impression that disregards points of detail.

Modern editions of the Greek texts derive from manuscripts, and their editors attach a commentary that is dedicated to clarifying the meaning of the language, but which may also offer suggestions about performance. Some translations carry commentaries, but others do not, and only very rarely does any editor or translator spell out fully his or her understanding of the performance conditions for tragedy or comedy. So, in general, it is best to expect to piece together a theatrical appreciation of a script oneself, taking advantage of any help that is available from commentaries or criticism, but expecting to do much of the work through a process of observation and what we might call deduction.

There are several approaches that will help to shape a preliminary map of an ancient script as a work for the theater. One of the simplest means to gain a sense of theatricality is to do what any modern stage manager might do on receiving a script, and that is to list the properties required for the action. These lists will reveal that tragedy is relatively sparing in its use of properties, which correspondingly may carry a high degree of significance, while comedy luxuriates in objects, but rarely attributes more than a temporary value to them. But any reliable stage manager will also have to know when a property is required, who is using it, where it is located at any time, and how frequently it is in operation throughout the play. This kind of mapping directs attention to action, and it may easily lead us to look closely at the manipulation of objects by characters in the script, and to see how objects are involved in transactions between characters.

A similar approach can be applied to costumes and masks in their contribution to the definition of characters. Mapping the age, gender, and status (which may include issues of slave and free, Greek and non-Greek, or distinctions of class amongst the free) of characters and chorus will help to establish a sense of some of the important tensions operating in the play. For this purpose, it is not essential to have a firm view of what specific costumes may have looked like, but to accept specific indications in the script where these exist, or to attribute (as a modern designer would) a suitably distinctive costume to the character in a vision of performance. Similarly, a sense of age, gender and status can be applied to the set of masks required for the performance of any script, whether those masks are conceived in the mind's eye according to their likely format in the fifth century, or on the basis of any alternative inspiration that will retain the characteristics of a set. There may at times be hints or indications in the scripts of what a particular mask may have looked like, but achieving a sense of a set is a constructive activity even without that help.

Securing a good sense of status, relations or relationships, and even of identity is a sound preliminary step to a more detailed appreciation of the actions and tensions of tragedy. Some scripts will establish these components of the drama without difficulty, but there are potential confusions and obscurities. To take one example, the character of Creon represents the same mythical figure in Sophocles' *Antigone, Oedipus the King,* and *Oedipus at Colonus,* namely the brother of Jocasta, both the uncle and the brother-in-law of Oedipus, and simultaneously the uncle and great-uncle of the children of Oedipus. But the Creon in Euripides' *Medea* is not the same mythical figure, and neither of these Creons is related or connected in any way to Creousa in Euripides' *Ion,* as their names might suggest. In many cases, the speaking characters of a tragedy will also need to be linked carefully to those other mythical figures to whom reference is made in the course of the action, since we are inevitably restoring knowledge that was held by the original culture. For Aristophanic comedy, the only reliable approach is to look closely at the social (or ethnic) status of each speaking or silent character, and relate that to the situation, since immediate family relations and relationships, although of considerable significance, often affect only a limited number of the roles. The total dependency of slaves on those who owned them, their loyalties, fears, or resentment, and their confinement to physical labors—which in the case of women may well be sexual—should form part of this preliminary mapping both of tragedies and comedies, as it may also inform any developed interpretations.

In the tragedies of Aeschylus, it is noticeable that characters regularly speak and respond to the chorus, and the centrality of the presence of the chorus has to be acknowledged to understand a type of performance that is not primarily dependent on dialogue between characters. In both tragedy and comedy, many characters will have a relationship with the chorus as well as with other characters. In many cases, the chorus has a leading relationship with one character in particular, and much of the dynamic of the play will flow from the fluctuations in that relationship. This central dynamic will be affected by the introduction of other characters, to whom the chorus as well as leading characters will respond. Attending to these issues at an early point may well prevent a skewed vision of the play, or enhance our sense of the subtlety of the tension, so that we recognize (for example) that although Agamemnon is revered by the chorus in Aeschylus' *Agamemnon,* the continuing relationship throughout the drama is between Clytemnestra and the chorus; and that although the chorus shows sympathy for Antigone in Sophocles' *Antigone,* the continuing and increasingly unstable relationship is between Creon and the chorus. In Aristophanic comedy, the chorus is normally either supportive of a leading character or vehemently and violently opposed to him or her: a divided chorus allows for both of these aspects in parallel, as in *Lysistrata,* while the comic duo of father and son in *Wasps* evoke contrasting responses from the same chorus. These relationships of leading characters with the chorus are nearly always varied and changed by the course of the comic action, and to an extent may be said to form the core of the drama, as they do in many tragedies even after Aeschylus.

Finally, it will always be helpful to consider what a performer would have to do physically in enacting or embodying any role, how the actor might have used voice and movement, as well as to assess the role critically from the point of view of character. Determining the nature of the setting, and its significance as a constituent of the dramatic situation, depends to a great extent on an appreciation of the construction, organization and use of the playing space in the theater.

THE PLAYING SPACE

The playing space for early tragedy will have been the flat ground of an *orchestra*. With the construction of a *skene* in the theater of Dionysus, it is clear that some characters appear from it, and that characters may enter it. Reappearance and reentry are also common.

In principle, the chorus arrives in the playing space from one or both of the two side paths (*parodoi* or *eisodoi* in Greek), and only leaves the playing space at the end of the play. This convention is on occasions broken, with the chorus temporarily leaving the *orchestra* by a side path in a few plays; and in two other striking examples the chorus first appears from the scene building (Aeschylus' *Eumenides,* the third play of the *Oresteia* trilogy), or enters into it to reappear during the course of the action (Euripides' *Helen*).

How far the action of the plays was confined to the *orchestra* is problematic. Before the construction of a *skene,* and with no reference to a door, there is little alternative. In Aeschylus' *Persians* (472 B.C.), the Queen of Persia arrives in a chariot, and in the early plays most characters arrive in the playing space from "elsewhere," apparently from side paths. In these plays the presence of the chorus, especially when linked to a leading character bound to them by ties of respect or obligation, seems to act as

strongly as any other explicit information in a definition of lo-
cale. Characters appear to them, or with them, and may leave
them; but it is the intensity of their experience far more than any
impression of a closely defined space which controls our understanding of the action.

With the construction of a *skene,* this perhaps longstanding
convention is bound to be partly broken. From the earliest scenic tragedies in the *Oresteia* the existence of a building is clearly
marked, and the implications of residence are from then rarely
absent. Even in the case of a temple, which is a repeated setting
for tragedies, the introduction of the priestess or the god, or, in
the hands of Euripides, the temple attendant (in his *Ion*), ensures
a firm acknowledgment of the material presence of the scene
building. It may be temporarily ignored, or, as in the case of comedy, readily redefined; but its existence nonetheless becomes a
principal means of determining locality.

By the time of Menander, the *skene* had three doors, and regularly realized its capacity as a facade to unify the action between two neighboring houses. The conception linking all the
surviving plays of Menander is one of lateral connection: the
space outside the doors is public, and there is no communication
with a chorus. Characters remove themselves before the chorus
arrives to sing, and only reappear afterward.

The problem in determining a standard practice for scenic
performance in the fifth century has largely rested in the degree
of attraction that the body of surviving work is understood to
have to either the lateral convention (as in the works of Menander) that comes after it, or to the orchestral convention that clearly
precedes it.

As late in the fifth century as the production of Sophocles'
Philoctetes in 409 B.C., two characters open the play with no explicit reference to the scene building. They appear from a side
path together, and the opening lines, spoken by Odysseus, iden-

tify "this" as the shore of the island of Lemnos. A short time later, a search is started for the mouth of a cave that catches the sun, and one of the two finds it.

The compelling interpretation of this opening unites the play far more firmly with what I have termed the orchestral convention than with the urbane, "street-side" convention of Menander. There is really very little to suggest, in any one of the surviving dramas of the fifth century, that the action of a play was confined to the immediate physical background of the facade presented by the scene building.

Tragedy repeatedly makes use of what are obviously the main doors of a scene building. With the existence of an *ekkuklema,* certain actors who are prone (such as Heracles in Euripides' tragedy of that name) must lie on it. Those who appear beside the corpses it regularly carries may stand on it, once it has projected from the *skene,* or, alternatively, they may come forward, to argue to (or with) the chorus. Proximity is not always to be assumed in the Greek theater, and if assumed it may still vary widely in what was a massive playing space. Nor should appearance from the scene building presuppose a rooting to the spot. Clytaemestra appears to welcome Agamemnon, in an address to the chorus, in *Agamemnon,* the first play of the *Oresteia.* But Agamemnon has arrived in a chariot, and has not set foot from it. We need not suppose that she shouted to them all from a distance.

Comedy regularly redefines its playing space in the course of a play. So in *Acharnians* by Aristophanes, the setting is first of all on Pnyx hill in Athens, with doubtless the audience cast in their other capacity as political assembly. But the setting fluently shifts to the house and home of the leading character, understood to be in "the country," since he proceeds immediately to celebrate the rural festival of Dionysus. Our scripts as records of performance can be awkward to read, for as a rule there are no original stage directions in them. But properties, people, and even painted indications of setting may all be removed in the space that, for us, separates one line from another.

The details of the action of any play may need to be deduced, and the scripts provide a wealth of detail on occasions. But they were not composed for deduction, and deduction can encounter the most frustrating obstacles. In Aristophanes' *Wasps,* all seems well. The old man, who is trapped in the *skene,* with the doors barred and a net stretched over it, tries to escape from a window. He has previously appeared on the roof, attempting to escape through the chimney; and our sense of the deployment of the *skene,* if not of its exact shape and appearance, is very strong in this play. But once he starts to climb down from the window, the indications in the script of physical activity become obscure (lines 430–60). It is clear that he is finally caught and held; that someone is instructed to climb up another way and beat him back; but who is where when, whether there is another window, when he is caught, all of which must have been exact in performance and obvious in presentation, are questions that cannot be immediately answered with any great confidence.

Some action will always have occurred by the door. For comedy, other problems remain. There is only one house and one pair of doors (a double door is almost certainly entailed by the existence of an *ekkuklema*) in Aristophanes' *Wasps,* performed in 422 B.C. One year later, with the production of Aristophanes' *Peace* in 421 B.C., sees scholars suggesting a radically different picture of the *skene,* in anticipation of the form with three doors available to Menander a century later. Tragedy, without exception it seems, used only one (central) door. The use of two (on either side of a third) or three doors is a presupposition for comedy in the later period, and seems so firmly attached to the comic form that it is likely to be an invention of it. Aristophanes' *Women in Assembly* of the early fourth century dramatizes neighbors. With a wooden *skene,* even above stone foundations, adaptations are possible.

The comedies of Aristophanes after *Peace* and before *Women in Assembly* (*Birds, Lysistrata, Women at the Thesmophoria,* and *Frogs*) show absolutely no dependence on three doors. Either construction preceded persistent realization, or what confronts us in these plays of Aristophanes is evidence of a tendency that only finally dictated to permanent construction. There is no easy answer; but it must remain indisputable that the conception of most plays in the fifth century required only one entrance, which could on occasions be redefined in the course of a play.

THE AUDIENCE

There is contradictory and confusing evidence on the composition of the audience for the dramatic festivals. The capacity of the *theatron* will have varied with its gradual extension, but a figure of between ten and fourteen thousand seems a reasonable generalization.

Athenian society in this period was conscious of quite firm categories, and amongst these adult citizen males held a dominant place in political, legal, military, and domestic affairs. Women were excluded from most aspects of public life, and slaves were regarded as one category of "things owned" by those who were "free." A large class of residents was formed by the "metics" (*metoikoi*), those Greeks who were immigrants to Athens or who were not of Athenian descent, and who did not have the full rights of citizens. It is perfectly possible that there were no rules affecting or controlling attendance at the theater, but the likelihood must be that of all the categories Athenian women and slaves would be the least in evidence. Visiting non-Athenians, particularly those acting as representatives of allied states, would have been present at the City Dionysia.

Athenian democracy, which was established at the end of the sixth century, and fully confirmed by the time of the *Oresteia*, attributed power to the people (*demokratia* combines "people," *demos,* with the concept of "power," *kratos,* in one word) in two decisive ways. The *demos* was effectively understood to be the totality of adult citizen males, and this body met in the political assembly (*ekklesia*) on the hill called Pnyx in Athens, to decide what we should call matters of state (*ta politika* in Greek, matters affecting the *polis,* or city/state), often with a strong military bias. The democracy also provided law courts, *dikasteria,* at which a representative selection of citizens would be the final arbiters in a majority of legal decisions.

It is important to realize that both these vital sectors of the political form taken by Athenian democracy relied on public speaking to a large audience, with a view to persuading a majority. The courts were composed regularly of five hundred *dikastai,* or jurymen, and attendance at the political assembly was supposed to be an obligation for all adult citizens. "Hearing," with a view to final judgment, was of the essence of Athenian democracy, and urgent persuasion the objective of public speaking. In this respect the shape of the political assembly is of considerable relevance in any accurate assessment of the activity of theater, and I have included diagrams of it (figs. 4a and 4b). A gently sloping embankment of different orientations in different periods was created to facilitate the reception and identification of speakers, and the analogies with the theater are plain (figs. 3a, 3b with 4a, 4b). Conversely, theaters were on some occasions, particularly during times of political instability, used as political meeting places. The connection between the theater and political life was far closer in Athenian life than it has been in modern times.

The expectations, reactions, tastes, feelings, and judgment of a relatively well-known audience of predictable scope must have affected the composition of plays to a very high degree. The allocation of prizes in the dramatic competitions seems to have worked by immediate and probably vociferous public pressure on a panel of ten judges, only finally selected just before the

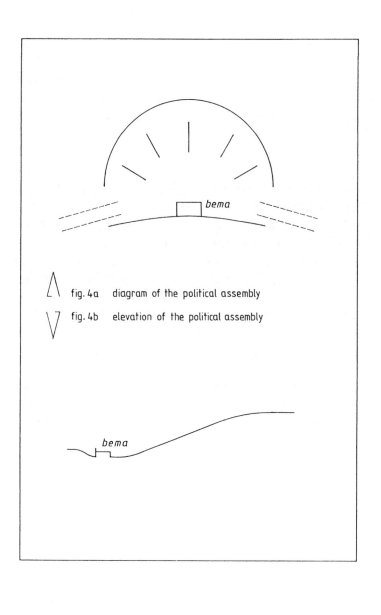

fig. 4a   diagram of the political assembly

fig. 4b   elevation of the political assembly

contest. From the verdicts of these men a majority was apparently achieved by a random selection of five out of ten. The procedure was clearly designed to safeguard the decisions from dishonest external influence. Some of the results of this system are known, and provide part of a picture of the general critical reaction. Aristophanes was disappointed by the audience reaction and the decision of the judges in relation to *Clouds,* which he proceeded to revise, commenting in the revision that he had seen the first version as intellectually the most "sophisticated" of his comedies. The text that survives of *Clouds* is a revision which was never presented, and which itself makes reference to the first production. Sophocles is said always to have been placed first or second in the tragic competition, but never third; Euripides won very few victories; and the Athenians voted a decree after the death of Aeschylus permitting reproduction of his tragedies in the place of new work. These judgments are interesting; but they leave us with only the barest indications of emotive response, or of the usual or varying criteria for critical appreciation or disapproval over the century. A comic distortion of critical judgment is presented by Aristophanes in his *Frogs* of 405 B.C., following the death of Euripides; but the contest in the underworld between Aeschylus and Euripides is simply and consistently irreverent, when it is not sentimental.

If it is impossible to determine with any accuracy what the Athenians thought or felt in detail about any play on any particular occasion, there are nonetheless some general controls on a modern assessment of what was presented to them. Two examples taken from the fabric of social life will illustrate this well. Athenian democracy gave a remarkable emphasis to the initiatives and obligations of the *kyrios* (literally "master"), the adult male who was legally responsible for all his dependants, and who was effectively the element of political and public life. A great deal of surviving Athenian drama reflects an interest in the *oikos* ("household"), seen as subject to the control of the *kyrios;* and a permeation of this concern into a world shaped by myth or fantasy provides much of the tension or humor apparent in many plays.

The second example is material, rather than thematic. The design of the larger Greek houses was traditionally based around an *aule,* or courtyard, from which entrances opened into the various parts of the house. The central doors of the *skene* are clearly taken to represent the main door to the courtyard in many plays where a "palace," or larger private house, is involved. Characters can often be assumed not to pass others—nor even, in some cases, to know what is happening in a different part of the house—when they go through them. A temple would also be understood to have sizable interior divisions of space, familiar in some form to most of the audience, and which could include some areas inaccessible to all but the cult priest/esses. This expands our conception of interior space in these plays, to an extent that would clearly not be so significant when the *skene* represented an inhabited cave, or a military tent.

Between the modern reader and the ancient script lies the audience for which it was composed. This is not an insuperable barrier, but as many adjustments as possible should be made before any "reading" is allowed to become completely convincing. Of all these, perhaps the most telling is that of repeated military activity as an inevitable definition of the adult male, and as a potential and catastrophic influence on the lives of others.

DELIVERY

Of all the aspects of the actor's technique in the Athenian theater, that of delivery stands out as being thoroughly characteristic of a convention which relied heavily on the voice. The absence of facial expression made increased attention to voice and gesture inevitable, and confirmed a major distinction from standard forms of public address, in the political assembly or in the law courts. But despite this crucial difference, the analogies between the three forms were striking, and theoretical writers applied a term derived from the existence of acting to the projection that should be given to speeches, which they called *hypokrisis*.

There are no handbooks on the actor's technique, nor is anything known of rehearsals. But it is possible to mark out from the scripts certain fairly clear signs of the demands placed on a performer by the particular convention.

In Aeschylus' *Agamemnon* Clytaemestra eventually reappears from the *skene* to display the corpses of Agamemnon and Cassandra, whom she has murdered. At this point, she takes pride in announcing that the achievement of what she had intended may now be revealed in stark contrast to the manner of her previous statements (lines 1372–79). Earlier in the play, she has greeted Agamemnon with an effusive speech of welcome, assembled from exaggerated flattery and a pretense of extreme concern for his safety (lines 855–913). Its extent had drawn an ironic comment from her husband, who said that her speech had equaled his absence, because both were very long (lines 914–16).

The most likely conclusion to be drawn from this sequence would be that in the original performance the actor was expected, and the script of the earlier speech drafted, to convey exaggeration and insincerity. The bearings suggested by this example can be confirmed by another. In Euripides' *Medea,* a woman character is again faced by the need to convince, and eventually deceive, a leading male character. Medea actively pleads with Creon, who is the king of the city in which she is resident, for a temporary reprieve from exile for herself and her children (lines 271–356). After Creon has granted her wishes and left, she acknowledges to the chorus that her behavior toward him was a form of flattery, designed to gain her ends and with a firm intention in mind. This intention proves to be the triple murder of Creon, his daughter, and her husband Jason (lines 364–85).

The activity of significant and extended deception allows for some of the clearest effects in the construction of Athenian tragedy, and was presumably intended and scripted for execution. The absolute alternative to active and acknowledged deception might be best seen in the sincerity of feeling which can be occasioned by deception. In Sophocles' *Electra,* Electra is given every reason to believe in the death of her brother, whose "ashes" are conveyed to her in an urn. The demonstration of her grief, which is extended (lines 1126–70), must provide for the play an extreme of sincere emotion, which stands in marked opposition to the hypocrisies determined by Aeschylus for Clytaemestra.

Most speeches, if not all, invite discrimination from the audience. Many are concerned with self-justification, because the figures seen are largely responsible for their actions, or, at least, for their immediate decisions. The portrayal of extreme sincerity or its opposite may have been one objective of the actor's technique, but there will have been others. In Sophocles' *Antigone,* the new king Creon appears from the *skene* to address the chorus. Before confirming the rigor of his recent proclamation forbidding the burial of his nephew Polyneices, killed one day earlier when attacking his own city, Creon is at pains to emphasize the continuing loyalty to the ruling house of Thebes of this élite of older citizens. They represent a tradition of respect and support across three generations of rulers already, he claims; they will, he imagines, support and respect him too, even in his early judgments. The proclamation in itself has demonstrated Creon's desire not to be thought to favor those close to him on his accession to power; and the delivery of this opening speech confirms his insecurity. On first public appearance, he is demonstrably willing to flatter those on whom he may have to rely to sustain him against public pressure (lines 162–222).

Of all the forms of delivery which may seem most obvious to the modern reader that of the portrayal of anger might encourage the greatest certainty. Words for anger are pointed in the script, and an accumulation of insult can offer firm signs of its presence in delivery. So in the exchange between Creon and Teiresias, the blind prophet, which occurs later in the same tragedy by Sophocles, the insults of Creon leveled at Teiresias prompt a slow rise to a prophecy of destruction directed at the king—as Teiresias himself acknowledges—like an arrow from a bow. The growth in intensity in clearly marked stages, and under explicit provocation, is in this case almost decreed by the composition of the script (lines 1033–90).

But two further examples from the same play offer interesting insights into the control that composition seems to place on delivery. In the opening exchange between Antigone and Ismene, two sisters whose diverse reactions to Creon's proclamation form the introduction to the action of the play, the intensity of conflict

only certainly includes the direct expression of anger at its climax, when Ismene refers to the "heated" resolution of her sister
(line 89). And later, at the first suggestion of opposition to his au-
thority, and of the possibility that contravention of his proclamation may have been the result of intervention by a god, Creon
orders the chorus to be silent, before they fill him with anger by
further developing that suggestion (line 280). These examples
are a warning that conclusions about delivery should be moni-
tored by a sense of dramaturgy, and the dynamic of exchanges.
Production and direction, and the full implications of composition, will have been as significant as any striking possibilities for
immediate expression on the part of the performer.

In comedy, certain conclusions present themselves as almost
inevitable, though since they are dependent on comparison they
remain poorly defined. Aristophanes' *Women at the Thesmophoria*
makes particularly heavy use of the technique of parody, deployed
by Aristophanes in a variety of forms, but rarely when a surviving song or tragedy permits us a direct comparison (see the section "Parody" below). In *Women at the Thesmophoria,* a relative of
the tragedian Euripides has infiltrated the women's religious festival identified in the title in order to defend Euripides from at-
tacks the women will make on the subject matter of his plays.
The relative is discovered and caught, and he and Euripides act
out "escape" motifs from some of the playwright's tragedies. By
chance, one of these ridiculous adaptations, or parodies, is from
Euripides' *Helen,* a surviving play. This permits a comparison
with the original, but more usefully for any understanding of
delivery it draws attention to what must have been a particular
resource of comic technique: a manner of indicating a certain
type of tragic delivery while unmistakably rendering its ridiculous opposite. It also provides some confirmation that the male
tragic performer will have modified his voice in representing
women. The relative of Euripides is a man who has disguised

himself as a woman to gain access to the festival. In representing Helen he can accomplish a parody of the tragic actor's realization of a woman as well as of the tragedy. This kind of vocal control may have been familiar from tragedy: the most likely division of roles for Sophocles' *Women of Trachis,* for example, would attribute the parts of both Deianira and Heracles to the same performer, which suggests disciplined flexibility rather than specialization.

A further point of comparison for the techniques of delivery in comic performance lies in its use of characters drawn from contemporary life. This not only provided some interesting activity for the mask maker, but posed problems for the playwright and the actor. Euripides was alive when Aristophanes represented him in his comedies *Acharnians* and *Women at the Thesmophoria,* and so was Socrates for the original production of *Clouds* in 423 B.C. But in respect to portrayal, and particularly to delivery, a more significant example is provided by the active political speaker Cleon, who is represented as the Paphlagonian slave in Aristophanes' *Knights.* What is interesting for our understanding of delivery in this play is that Cleon is known from another, reliably descriptive source (the historian Thucydides) to have been the "most violent" of contemporary public figures, and the most persuasive speaker. It is not unlikely that this description will have referred as much to his manner, his delivery in the assembly and elsewhere, as it did to his policies; and Aristophanes certainly chooses to represent him in that way, as far as the comments and expectations of other characters in *Knights* permit us to judge. The details of performance remain obscure, but the intention will surely have entailed some representation by the performer, as one of the varieties of comic distortion.

One final observation should concern the descriptive reports given to messengers in tragedy. These extended speeches are often climactic, by their position in the play and by construction.

A spoken description of major events will have been important in antiquity, and a vivid evocation often admired, perhaps best by those not directly affected, or by those immensely relieved by the news conveyed. Speeches of this kind in tragedy suggest a capacity for recall which should not be doubted in a society of this kind; and their subjects—disastrous accidents, a scene of explosive individual violence, or some part of the scale of a military engagement, to take three examples—are not unlikely topics for detailed descriptions. The composition and delivery of them in tragedy are artifices, as is often their contrived effect on a character carefully placed by the playwright to absorb their impact. The artifice will have been recognized by the audience; but it should not be assumed, in a modern reading, to have diminished their original theatrical excitement.

DISTANCE
& PHYSICAL ACTION

Detailed stage directions are substantially an invention of the nineteenth century, and the scripts of ancient drama are a record of the words. But taken by themselves, the scripts still give some quite precise indications of physical action and of the use of space.

Direct physical contact firmly placed in the playing space provides a starting point for analysis, in either an embrace or a blow. In Aristophanes' *Frogs,* Dionysus and a slave, Xanthias, visit the underworld, and are alternately beaten by the ghastly doorkeeper of the palace of Hades, who is accompanied by slaves. All three speaking actors finally enter the *skene* (lines 605–73). The likelihood is that they are never far from the doors. By contrast, in Euripides' *Hecuba* the queen appears first from the tent of Agamemnon, which is the *skene,* leaning on a stick and supported by younger women as she moves slowly forward. In Euripides' *Heracles,* the name character is prostrate on the *ekkuklema* late in the play, next to the corpses of his wife and children. He covers his head with his cloak in shame at the approach of Theseus, who first instructs the third actor, playing Amphitryon, to unveil him, and then does so himself. Finally, in Euripides' *Ion,* the chorus has gathered close to the steps of the temple of Apollo represented by the *skene,* close enough to hear the sound of the doors opening. Wherever Ion may be standing, his supposed father then bursts out of the temple and attempts to embrace him. Ion is disgusted, pushes his hands away, and eventually threatens him with an arrow from the bow he is carrying (lines 517–24).

Prominent among other kinds of physical contact in tragedy are those moments when one character begs for a favor from another. In the exchange between Medea and Creon in Euripides' *Medea* (431 B.C.), Medea finally secures the reprieve she is seeking by a direct physical appeal to the king of Corinth, grasping his knees and perhaps then his hand (lines 324–56). This form of appeal is repeated by Euripides three years later, when in *Hippolytus* the nurse and companion to Phaedra first grasps her hand, and then falls to hold her knees in a successful attempt to learn from her the cause of her sickness (lines 324–36). At moments of this kind the immediate space between the performers is clearly defined, but their position in the wider playing space is left open to question. The problem facing the visual reconstruction of tragedy is to reconcile these two different areas.

Two further examples may go some way toward doing this. At the opening of Sophocles' *Oedipus the King,* what seems to be a large group of suppliants, composed of young children, old people, priests, and young men, has gathered close to the altars outside the palace of Oedipus, to appeal for his help against the plague. Oedipus appears from the palace to speak to them, and the exchange between him and the Priest of Zeus is finally curtailed by a signal from others placed further away that the third performer, as Creon, is approaching along a side path. Creon is seen to have a garland on his head, and is then within hailing distance of the king.

A similar kind of approach by Polyneices in Sophocles' *Oedipus at Colonus* introduces a third component of physical setting, open to a less close definition than contact or extreme distance, but vital to the action of many plays. Oedipus, old, blind, and homeless, has been carefully placed by the chorus in the early part of the play on a seat of rocks well away from a wooded sanctuary dedicated to the Eumenides. He finds himself physically incapable of unaided movement (lines 501–2) and exhausted, and cannot be parted from the proximity of sanctuary.

Oedipus' daughters are grouped with him in this position as Polyneices makes his approach from a side path. He is seen at a distance by Antigone, is identified, and finally stands close enough to the actor playing Oedipus to describe his clothing and the details of his mask. He hesitates to address Oedipus directly, and speaks to his sisters instead, attempting to use them as intermediaries. His father turns away: they eventually speak to each other, but there are no indications of direct physical contact. The appeal that passes, at this close distance, from Polyneices to Oedipus is vehemently rejected (lines 1249–1413).

This kind of controlled proximity provides some of the most elusive problems in visualizing the action of ancient tragedy. Polyneices is held at a close separation from Oedipus that corresponds to the conflict between his need to make the appeal and his hesitation—and perhaps his revulsion—before the disfigured and ghastly old man, who is his brother as well as his father. Revulsion may take a different form: in Sophocles' *Philoctetes,* Philoctetes' wound seeps and is obnoxious, and his original isolation on the island of Lemnos was caused, at least in part, by disgust from others at the smell of it. But the whole action of Sophocles' play, which sees Neoptolemus sent to stay by him in the hope of stealing his bow, or of removing the man himself, is presented as a set of variations on the conflict between the impulse of approach and a sense of revulsion, of hesitation, or of suspicion that repeatedly acts to hold both men back. Extreme distance and immediate contact are the simplest deductions for a modern reader, but the tension of tragedy will have been regularly expressed in the careful description of an area enclosing two (or three) performers.

For comedy, the problems are of a different kind. Comic action is just that—active humor—and much of it is located around the doors of the *skene,* or in a close relationship to them. The wider playing space is represented by interaction of performers—often violent—with the chorus, or by an almost ritual expulsion of other performers/characters, who are often introduced in succession along the side paths. The relationship to the skene of a similar physical concept may vary within an apparently slight range. For the opening of both *Clouds* and *Wasps,* two figures are trying to sleep outside. The two slaves of *Wasps* are placed close to the door, because they are supposed to be guarding it and not falling asleep. The two prone figures in *Clouds* are Strepsiades and his son, who eventually discuss a door which is at some distance. The revised text of the play seems to conceive of them as being at first "inside," and then later at a distance practicable for an approach to the school of Socrates. The slaves in *Wasps,* if they are to avoid being caught out and seen dozing by their owner, must keep close to the doors, because their owner is placed on the roof.

Other kinds of distance determine themselves effectively without the need for exactitude. Comedies, and comic routines, often compose themselves around objects, and one favorite device consists of the repetition of fetching a succession of thematically related objects from inside the *skene* out through the doors to a performer or performers firmly located outside. In *Acharnians,* a contrast is achieved between the self-indulgence of Dikaiopolis and the hard military life of Lamachus by having brought to each on order the equipment and provisions for a meal and for a military campaign respectively (lines 1071–1149). The two performers finally leave down side paths, so they will have been at a distance from the doors and presumably separated. In *Lysistrata*, Kinesias is seen and then identified from the scene building, approaching along a side path. He appeals to his wife to come down to him from the *skene*, and invites her to make love with him on the ground. The rest of the scene sees her teasing his frustration by continually entering the *skene* to bring out further comforts or enticements, which he claims he does not need. The routine is again repetition, and the action will have taken place at a sufficient distance from the doors for the visual effect of interruption to be registered successfully (lines 829–979). Kinesias finally leaves along a side path.

A larger number of performers may gather around an object in a grouping only loosely connected with any definition given by the scene building. In *Lysistrata* and *Women in Assembly*, Aristophanes repeats the idea of a conspiracy of women in a public space. In the first comedy, unity is provided by the wine-pouring as a preliminary to taking an oath of sexual abstinence; and in the second, individuals practice the speeches they will make in the assembly by passing the speaker's wreath from one to another. Both meetings are called at dawn, and in both plays the *skene* is almost immediately used to justify the appearance of one of the conspirators. But in *Lysistrata* it is finally defined as the gate to the *akropolis*, and then approached and entered by some of the performers; while in *Women in Assembly* it retains its definition as a house for the following scene, as the women leave to go to the assembly. A central position for both groups, which are formed with one exception by approaches from the side, seems most likely; and perhaps for this reason the *skene* itself is temporarily ignored until its chosen redeployment.

CHORAL SONG
& CHORAL ACTION

Some forms of comic and tragic action draw performers into close involvement with a chorus which is extremely active, and which may dominate the playing space. This is particularly true of early tragedy, and of comedy. The standard assumption about the chorus is that it sings and dances. This covers a wide range of theatrical possibilities.

Not enough is known about the choral music of Greek antiquity to make a reconstruction of its theatrical value possible. The same is unfortunately true of dance, for the occasional illustration of members of a dancing chorus (plate 1) is obviously inadequate to picture a sequence, though some vases clearly do attempt to give a picture of dance steps or movements (plates 2 and 3). But some observations can be made on the construction of the choral song, and its involvement in the action of a play may be explicit.

A typical tragic choral song might be composed in five parts, on the system a^1, a^2, b^1, b^2, c. These systems are detected in the existing scripts by the fact that the organization of the verse meter corresponds for two parts (a^1, a^2), and then changes for the next two. The system may extend, and the internal length of the parts of it may vary. It may or may not be concluded by a part standing in isolation (c). The corresponding parts of a song are conventionally known as *strophe* (literally "turning") and *antistrophe* ("turning back"); but the original significance of these terms may well be musical, rather than choreographic. This is certainly the implication of a passage mocking musical composition (for tragedy) in Aristophanes' *Women at the Thesmophoria* (lines 66–69).

A good example of this kind of tragic song is represented by an ode (the Greek word for "song") in Euripides' *Hippolytus* (lines 525–64). The action of the play has seen the revelation of Phaedra's passion for Hippolytus, her stepson, and the initial shock felt by the nurse giving way to a plan on her part to cure Phaedra of this sickness.

The song exists in four parts (a¹, a², b¹, b²) without the conclusion (c), and opens with a prayer to Eros, the personification of the impetus of passion, which occupies the first two parts (a¹, a²—lines 525–44). The second two parts (b¹, b²—lines 545–64) consist of examples taken from mythology of the drastic power of Aphrodite, the goddess identified with sexuality, to strike the lives of women violently. The whole song concludes, in the final lines of its fourth part, with an image, comparing the potent universality of Aphrodite to the flight of a bee (lines 563–64).

strophe

Love distills desire upon the eyes,	525
love brings bewitching grace into the heart	
of those he would destroy.	
I pray that love may never come to me	
with murderous intent,	
in rhythms measureless and wild.	
Nor fire nor stars have stronger bolts	530
than those of Aphrodite sent	
by the hand of Eros, Zeus' child.	

antistrophe
In vain by Alpheus' stream,   535
in vain in the halls of Phoebus' Pythian shrine
the land of Greece increases sacrifice.
But Love the King of Men they honor not,   540
although he keeps the keys
of the temple of desire,
although he goes destroying through the world,
author of dread calamities
and ruin when he enters human hearts.

strophe
The Oechalian maiden who had never known   545
the bed of love, known neither man nor marriage,
the Goddess Cypris gave to Heracles.
She took her from the home of Eurytus,
maiden unhappy in her marriage song,
wild as a Naiad or a Bacchanal,   550
with blood and fire, a murderous hymenaeal!

antistrophe
O holy walls of Thebes and Dirce's fountain   555
bear witness you, to Love's grim journeying:
once you saw Love bring Semele to bed,
lull her to sleep, clasped in the arms of Death,
pregnant with Dionysus by the thunder king.   560
Love is like a flitting bee in the world's garden
and for its flowers, destruction is in his breath.
{TRANSLATION BY DAVID GRENE, IN
THE COMPLETE GREEK TRAGEDIES}

The opening prayer (a¹) is clearly motivated by the recent understanding of Phaedra's passion, and takes a common form of a

negative wish, that Eros may not strike the chorus badly, or out of rhythm (lines 528–29), which serves as a religious acknowledgment of the divinity of the power of Eros, joined to that of Aphrodite. Continuity in the second part (a^2) follows easily from the matching meter: Eros is a divinity of great destructive potency, and it is futile for organized religion not to institute his worship. The understanding here is that rites of worship, commonly expressed in the sacrifice which links human to divine, are an effective appeasement of an immortal power. The second two parts (b^1, b^2), which share a metrical pattern which is distinct from that of the first pair, though closely related to it, provide two separate examples: the one of Deianira (the Oechalian maiden) in a sexual union born of violence (b^1), and the second of Semele, who was destroyed by a thunderbolt in childbirth (b^2). The stories of both women formed part of the repertoire of tragic myth, from which other surviving plays were composed (Sophocles' *Women of Trachis,* and, less directly, Euripides' *Bacchae*).

The structure of this song, which works through development as well as balance, its subject matter, and the timing of its intervention in the action of the play are all accessible; and with considerable variation it provides a comprehensible pattern for an integration of choral lyric into a modern reading of the tragedies. But the diversity of lyric is immense; and apart from the knowledge that choral song was accompanied by a piper (*auletes*) playing double pipes, regularly pictured on vases (e.g., *DFA,* fig. 35), our ignorance of its music and dance is a definitive limitation. Musical mode and melody, physical expression by the use of hands and arms, and varieties of dance step or scheme are all attested; but what is known of them hardly permits even a reasonable generalization for the fifth century. Appropriate distinctions were almost certainly made for tragedy, comedy, and satyr play, and these were presumably familiar to the audience by convention.

The existence of meter, and its explicit organization into schemes in the scripts, can easily dominate a consideration of the chorus. But there is an abundance of evidence in the plays which points to a remarkable fluidity in the deployment of the chorus as a body, which for discussion is perhaps best separated from the internal design of a song. The plays of Aeschylus seem to provide evidence of an extremely active chorus, easily defined as apprehensive (*The Persians*), simply terrified (*Seven against Thebes* and *The Suppliant Maidens*), or combative and violent (*The Eumenides,* the third play of the *Oresteia*). The fluidity of movement in these plays can often only be guessed, partly because of the extent of the choral part(s) in them, which is noticeably greater than that standard for the later tragedies of Sophocles and Euripides. Combative violence is also a characteristic of comic choruses in Aristophanes, and it is tempting to see comedy as more traditional than tragedy in its preservation of dramatic agitation in the orchestral playing space to a far later date. In this respect, a general scheme of the broadest relevance can be provided by a contrast between the involvement of the chorus in the activity of the play in Euripides' *Bacchae* and in Aeschylus' *Eumenides*. Both plays dramatize a ritual hunt of a leading male character by a female group, inspired by a religious force and intending to kill. In *The Eumenides,* the hunt is performed by the chorus; in *The Bacchae,* the hunt takes place outside the playing space and is not performed by the chorus, although they are devotees of the god concerned, who is Dionysus. They remain in the playing space, and their songs express a combination of religious intensity and vicarious excitement, in the anticipation or reception of acts initiated by others.

The Eumenides provides a good example of choral action. The chorus first appears from the *skene* itself and apparently singly. The full group is composed still close to the *skene* when they are banished from the temple it represents by the god of the sanctuary, Apollo. They leave the *orchestra,* go down a side path, and arrive back again in the playing space, in an enactment of a successful search for the actor playing Orestes. This series of actions is expressed verbally, in both speech and song.

The exact location of the chorus in the playing space is nearly always hypothetical, and often dependent on the location of an actor or actors with whom the chorus is immediately involved. The search for Orestes in *The Eumenides,* for example, may range through the *orchestra* and culminate by the *skene,* where he is discovered. We deduce his presence there from the statue of the goddess Athene which he is clasping in the hope of asylum, since the statue may very well be located on the *ekkuklema* in front of the *skene* doors. The problem can be usefully seen in Euripides' *Suppliant Women.* At the opening of the play one actor is lying, collapsed, at the doorway of the temple represented by the *skene.* With him is a group of children. A second actor is apparently sitting by an altar, or altars, and surrounded, in what is explicitly stated to be a circle, by the chorus. The full theatrical complement is then completed by the arrival of the third actor, along a side path, who seems to see the choral group first and the actor and boys in the porch later, though this sequence may not be significant. The disposition of the performers clearly indicated in the script points to an orchestral location for the altar, and our visual and spatial sense of this scene is particularly strong.

For comedy, a link to the tragic chorus is provided in the hunt or search, which also seems to have been a regular activity for the satyric chorus. In a large number of later plays, and in part in the tragedies of Aeschylus, the arrival of the chorus, with chant or song, is motivated by an attraction to the location as defined by the *skene,* or to a particular character either known or expected to be in the playing space. In Euripides' *Suppliant Women,* one extreme is represented because the script of the play opens as a description of the elaborate display in front of the audience.

The most likely conclusion here must be that when the players enter the playing space before the beginning of the scripted action, they will have done so in silence. The alternative extreme can be illustrated, in comedy, by the chorus for Aristophanes' *Acharnians,* who arrive in detestation and violent pursuit of a character whom they regard as a traitor. He has, in fact, escaped into the *skene,* and their initial search must cover the *orchestra,* after their approach has been forcibly established in advance by a character arriving at a run from a side path. The attack on the "traitor" takes place when he has reappeared from the *skene* and enacted a procession with members of his family. From the moment of attack, the family finds no further mention in the script. The procession, the disappearance of the family group and most of the properties they are carrying, and the isolation of the one main character, apparently prevented from reentering the *skene* or escaping along a side path, place the attack firmly in the *orchestra,* where the full scope of twenty-four performers threatening just one would be seen to best advantage.

In general, a close association of the chorus with the *orchestra* seems inevitable apart from moments of explicit reference to the *skene*—such as, for example, the entry of the chorus into it in Euripides' *Helen.* There is no clear understanding of the playing space, in continuity of design or conception, that can consistently locate choral song and action anywhere else. If this is the case, then interaction between chorus and characters must be visualized as drawing actors into the *orchestra* as readily as it draws chorus to actors initially or apparently located by the *skene.* How the chorus may have been dispersed in the *orchestra* when addressed by characters or involved, at least partially, in exchanges with or between them is another problem, which does not seem to be susceptible to generalization. The complete perimeter, particular areas within it, and the possibility of marked divisions of a chorus in the playing space, sometimes apparent in characterization (Aristophanes' *Lysistrata* has a divided chorus of old women and old men), are as likely as components of the total convention as any major, single grouping close to the *skene*. A chorus positioned here rapidly becomes theatrically implausible: it will have to pull back to sing and dance in the *orchestra,* and will interrupt or visually inhibit the transit of actors from *skene* to side path or the reverse.

The tradition that the tragic chorus sang in three linear ranks of five, constructed in a block formation, comes from later antiquity, and would appear to be contradicted by explicit indications in at least some of the scripts. It cannot be true of the first appearance of the chorus in *The Eumenides* (458 B.C.), and seems totally irreconcilable with the description of the "circle" in Euripides' *Suppliant Women* (later 420s B.C.). A similar construction for comedy also seems highly implausible as a general rule, and is explicitly contradicted in Aristophanes' *Women at the Thesmophoria* (lines 953–68) of 411 B.C. But there is no reason to suppose that the chorus for tragedy did not sing (and dance) in formation on appropriate occasions, perhaps even regularly so after its initial appearance (plate 1).

Certain sections of the script for the tragic chorus are differentiated metrically in a manner which does not indicate either song or the occasional involvement of chorus members in spoken exchanges between themselves or with actors. The usual assumption is that these passages were chanted, and there is at least a strong likelihood that they were accompanied by directional movement, rather than dance. Passages of this kind often introduce the chorus into the *orchestra,* and are then usually followed by the opening choral song. For comedy, a combination of short song with spoken or chanted harangue is repeated to form the *parabasis* of the chorus, which in its fullest form may have as a prelude a short call for attention, immediately followed by an extended (spoken or chanted) section which allows the poet to justify his work. Despite the strict formality of this sequence, and the certainty of accompaniment by the pipe player in some part (Aristophanes' *Birds,* lines 676–800), the scripts generally reveal little of its presentation.

An actor or actors may also be involved in a system of song and possibly dance with the chorus, and this, for example, reaches degrees of considerable complexity in Aeschylus' *Libation Bearers* (lines 306–478). Varieties of this form might be a chant from an actor combined with song from the chorus, or with chant from the chorus. These distinctions are often hard to follow in translations, which are weak in their notation of theatrically quite distinct elements.

The separation of parts of a song by spoken sections is a relatively unusual feature of tragedy but a regular assumption for comedy, and tragedy may also, on occasions, make use of a repeated refrain.

PARODY

The relation of comedy to tragedy is an integral feature of theatrical activity in the fifth century, because throughout most of the century in performances at the City Dionysia, and from just before 430 B.C. at the Lenaea, Athenians were accustomed to a close association of the two forms (see above, "The Organization of the Festivals").

The degree of contrast between tragedy and comedy is explicit in the use made by Aristophanes of parodies of tragic language, mechanisms, and situations. Comedy is crude and colloquial, as part of its direct appeal to an audience; and mock solemnity achieved by the inclusion of lines from tragedies, or by the imitation of tragic language, is an immediate source of laughter. This recurrent technique can be extended to a parody of scenes, first mentioned above in connection with *Women at the Thesmophoria* (see above, "Delivery"). In that play, Aristophanes takes advantage of two tragedies presented by Euripides one year earlier, *Helen* and *Andromeda,* to burlesque the idea of escape. The recall of lines, part lines, or groups of lines from Euripides' *Helen* is clear to us because that tragedy (unlike *Andromeda*) survives; and Aristophanes places them in an inevitably free version of the reunion of Menelaus and Helen, which is interspersed with incredulous interjections from a third party and padded out with appropriate pseudo-tragic language and gross distortions of his own. Later in the same play he adds a further parody of *Andromeda*, which includes what must be a distorted version of a solo song by Andromeda and the arrival of the rescuing hero (Perseus), suspended, apparently, from the *mechane*. In both parodies, Aristophanes' comic caricature of Euripides plays the part of "his" male principals, and the captured relative lives up to the dramatic implications of his impersonation of a woman at the women's festival of the title.

Aristophanes' fascination with Euripides, which sees him introducing the tragedian as a character in three of his surviving eleven plays (*Acharnians, Women at the Thesmophoria, Frogs*), absorbs a great deal of his interest in the comic potential of tragedy. His attention is sophisticated: a ruthless parody of Euripidean costume and properties in Acharnians; of the "idle" use of the *ekkuklema* in the same play; of the *mechane* in the opening of *Peace* and in the scene discussed above; and of technical aspects of composition (introductions and solo songs) in the contest between "Aeschylus" and "Euripides" in *Frogs*. In both *Women at the Thesmophoria* and *Frogs* the parodies form the substance of the second half of the comedy; and it is the theme of "Euripides" as tragic writer—deeply suspect for his portrayals of female characters, or nostalgically recalled after death—which forms the underlying conception of these comedies. The same is also true, in part, of *Acharnians,* in which Aristophanes seizes on certain striking characteristics of Euripides' *Telephos,* a lost tragedy performed thirteen years before *Acharnians,* to lend shape to his comic action. Telephos was the king of a region near Troy who was wounded in a preliminary action against the Greeks, and he is compelled to travel to Greece to get his wound healed. Although the substance of *Telephos* is lost, some fragments remain; and apart from parodies of costume (a king in rags) and direct or reported action (the seizure of a child as a hostage, parodied again in *Women at the Thesmophoria*), it is almost certain that the comically provocative defense of Spartan conduct given to Dikaiopolis in *Acharnians* reflects an attempt by Telephos to justify the self-defense of "barbarians" against the Greeks. The character of Lamachus, as the type of the general in *Acharnians* and a foil for Dikaiopolis, is also likely to be a parody of the type of the aggressive and single-minded Greek generals to whom Telephos delivered his plea. Similar uncompromising figures can be found by the modern reader in the characters of Agamemnon and Menelaus in Sophocles' *Ajax*, a tragedy which may have had an influence on Euripides' conception in *Telephos*.

It is, of course, true that parody in Aristophanes is not confined to Euripides. "Aeschylus" is a leading character in *Frogs*, in which there are parodies of his introductions and his choral songs, alongside allusive mockery of his concept of tragedy and techniques of plot construction. In *Women at the Thesmophoria*, the recently successful young tragedian Agathon is introduced as a character not only to mock his personality—the *ekkuklema* is used again, as is costume—but to present a parody of the style of his songs (lines 101–29). *Wasps* concludes with the irrepressible juror ProCleon demonstrating his capacity to outshine some forms of tragic and possibly satyric dance, ascribed to named performers. *Lysistrata* concludes with what pretends to be a parody of Spartan forms of song and dance. In *Acharnians*, Dikaiopolis, in a comic account of the causes of the current war between Athens and Sparta, provides an unmistakable parody of the mythical causes of conflict between Greeks and Persians expressed in the introduction to the contemporary *Histories* of Herodotus, a prose work undoubtedly recited or read at Athens (lines 496–556). In *Birds*, the airy location of the newly founded city is seen to be a suitable venue for the vanities and conceits of the dithyrambic poet Kinesias (lines 1372–1409).

Much of Aristophanic comedy is concerned with what is topical, and this in part explains the presence of what we would call theatrical, musical, or literary parody in many of the plays; even in *Frogs,* which has a retrospective quality, Euripides is only recently dead. But the character of Dionysus in *Frogs* refers to his own reading of a tragedy by Euripides (the play is *Andromeda,* performed seven years earlier). It is clear from this as from other evidence that literary texts, including plays, were available for purchase in Athens from about that time; and there must always have been at least an official or inherited private copy for our scripts to have survived. There is an obvious irony in this passage from *Frogs,* since "Dionysus," of all the gods, might well be thought to take an interest in the past products of his own competitions—and as a god to have access to a script. But it does seem likely that Aristophanes would have had more than an acute theatrical memory—whether visual or verbal—to help him in recalling the texts of tragedies. *Acharnians* was produced thirteen years after *Telephos,* and allusions to that play suggest that Aristophanes might expect a significant proportion of his audience to be familiar with its action.

But apart from reading, or a reliance on sharp memory encouraged by humor, there is also the possibility of a repeat production of the original tragedy. This was permitted by public decree (after his death) for the plays of Aeschylus: a remarkable measure that was presumably necessary for a breach of precedent at a major festival like the City Dionysia, where work otherwise had to be original. But in the case of other writers any reproduction in the fifth century would have had to take place at the many lesser festivals of Dionysus in the townships or districts of Attica, or in a location such as Piraeus, the port of Athens. There was a theater in Piraeus by at least the end of the century, and certainly at Thorikos, in the southeast of Attica, from a much earlier date. Competitions for actors were established at the major festivals during the course of the century, and these may well have encouraged the spread of dramatic performances outside the city center, increasing familiarity with some popular plays. A growing professionalism among actors, with related developments, might readily provide a background for the later revivals of old plays at the City Dionysia itself in the fourth century. An increasing emphasis on the professionalism and consequently the mobility of the actor is also a likely reason for the decline of the chorus, which is a marked feature of comedy at least in the fourth century.

But as a comic technique parody is not confined to theatrical or literary sources. The great opportunity which tragedy provided for comedy was that it was a parallel performance, easily recalled, which might at times give substantial shape to the related resources of comic theater. This characteristic—of a public performance—was shared by many features of public life, which, because Athenian institutions were for most of the fifth century democratic, were perhaps almost tediously familiar to a majority of the audience. The mimicry and mockery that comedy displays draw our attention at times to this tedium, and offer a relief from it. There are parodies of the formulas of the political assembly (*ekklesia*) at the introduction of the chorus in *Women at the Thesmophoria,* and of speechmaking at the assembly in the introduction to *Women in Assembly.* Placed alongside the extensive mockery of the diplomatic agenda of the *ekklesia* at the opening of *Acharnians,* these add up to a sophisticated and varied exploitation of the same, totally familiar institution. The procedures and apparatus of democratic justice receive a similar treatment in the trial of the dog in the central part of *Wasps,* and the trite formulas of oracles, produced and used for political purposes, are parodied heavily in episodes from *Knights, Peace,* and *Birds.* Ritual, in the form of oath swearing (as in the introduction to *Lysistrata*) or even rural celebration (the rural procession in honor of Dionysus in *Acharnians*), offers possibilities for distortion or exaggeration; and individual characters may themselves contain the seeds of formulas of behavior or verbal expression.

This is true of Lamachus, who is the type of the soldier-general in *Acharnians,* with his jargon and equipment, and perhaps equally true of "Socrates," presented in a comic distortion of the intellectual teacher (sophist), with his terminology and instruments, in *Clouds.* But it may also extend to a collection of types, gathered around a recognizable occasion. In *Birds,* the newly founded city in the air is disturbed by the arrival of intruders. They number a priest, a poet, an oracle-monger, a surveyor, an *episkopos* (an Athenian imperial officer), a man who sells copies of laws and decrees, a choral composer, and an informer. All might readily be associated with the foundation of the new settlement, established as it is by renegade Athenians; and the sight and sound of them, and an absolute rejection of them as intruders, constitute a large part of the second half of the play.

Parody is not a concept that applies as readily to tragedy. But not all tragedy is absolutely serious, and critics have rightly drawn attention to elements of comedy in all three surviving tragedians. Perhaps the most accessible of these scenes is that between the shipwrecked hero Menelaus and a hostile doorkeeper in Euripides' *Helen:* itself, ironically, parodied by Aristophanes in *Women at the Thesmophoria.* But we should also add the ridiculous and pathetic appearance of the Phrygian slave from the roof of the *skene* toward the end of Euripides' *Orestes,* and the dressing of Pentheus in women's clothing in *The Bacchae.* There are comic precedents for both these scenes. In *Wasps* there is an attempted escape from the *skene* by ProCleon, which occupies the introduction, and the "barbaric" language of the Scythian guard in *Women at the Thesmophoria* is to some degree echoed by the Phrygian slave. In both *The Bacchae* and *Women at the Thesmophoria* the careful clothing of a man is the preliminary to spying on women gathered in seclusion at a women's religious celebration. What evidence there is would seem to suggest that Euripides was as willing to create his own equivalent of parody in brilliant innovation for tragedy as was Aristophanes to mock him as innovator.

What the concept of parody when applied to tragedy may also allow us to do is to recognize conscious attempts at recall. The most famous of these lies in Euripides' radical transformation mation of the story of Electra in his tragedy of that name. Electra herself, in this play, refers directly and dismissively to techniques of recognition (of Orestes, her brother, by Electra) used by Aeschylus in *Libation Bearers;* and this has suggested to many the possibility of a reproduction of Aeschylus' trilogy, the *Oresteia,* shortly before the presentation of Euripides' play (about 420 B.C.). Euripides seems noticeably interested in the work of others: *The Bacchae* is, apparently, a reworking of a theme by Aeschylus, as is his *Suppliant Women* (of a lost trilogy by Aeschylus), as perhaps is his *Iphigenia at Aulis.* In *The Phoenician Women* the king Eteocles, in the climax to a review of strategic options with Creon, dismisses abruptly the idea of detailing the names of the captains who are to defend the seven gates of Thebes against impending attack (lines 751–52). In so doing, he removes from the audience the possibility of a repeat of virtually the whole dramatic substance of Aeschylus' surviving *Seven against Thebes.* In the same tragedy by Euripides, the introduction of the blind Teiresias to Creon and the subsequent scene recall strongly to us, and perhaps did to some of the Athenian audience, similar scenes between prophet and ruler in Sophocles' far earlier *Antigone* and *Oedipus the King* (*Phoenician Women,* lines 834–959). There is no explicit parody, but the familiarity that lies behind parody and the principle of reshaping for a sophisticated original purpose seem closely related. The connection goes further: the dismissive references that we hear from Euripides' Electra and Eteocles may confirm that Aristophanes was aware of "modernist" opinions on dramaturgy (held against Aeschylus) actually expressed by Euripides, which would account more than a little for the theme of *Frogs*.

But the key to parody must be found in the audience, and not in the playwright/composer alone. Familiarity with certain forms, either theatrical or institutional, with their presentation and the language appropriate to them, is clearly vital in sustaining and shaping both tragedy and comedy in the last quarter of the fifth century. The role of satyric drama in these relations is extremely hard to determine, except that the one complete surviving satyric play, Euripides' *Cyclops*, is obviously an adaptation of an episode narrated in detail in Book Nine of the epic poem the *Odyssey*, ascribed to Homer.

TRANSLATION
& ADAPTATION

Translation is, like theater itself, an art of presentation, and all translations bear the mark of their originators. Below are listed, as examples, some versions of the opening lines of Aeschylus' *Agamemnon;* they are spoken by the watchman.

Ye fav'ring gods, relieve me from this toil:
Fixed, as a dog, on Agamemnon's roof
I watch the live-long year, observing hence
The host of stars, that in the spangled skies
Take their bright stations, and to mortals bring
Winter and summer; radiant rulers, when
They set, or rising, glitter through the night.
{ROBERT POTTER}

This waste of year-long vigil I have prayed
God for some respite, watching elbow-stayed,
As sleuthhounds watch, above the Atreidae's hall,
Till well I know yon midnight festival
Of swarming stars, and them that lonely go,

Bearers to man of summer and of snow,
Great lords and shining, throned in heavenly fire.
{GILBERT MURRAY}

The gods it is I ask to release me from this watch
A year's length now, spending my nights like a dog,
Watching on my elbow on the roof of the sons of Atreus
So that I have come to know the assembly of the nightly stars
Those which bring storm and those which bring summer to men,
The shining Masters riveted in the sky—
I know the decline and rising of those stars.
{LOUIS MACNEICE}

I ask the gods some respite from the weariness
of this watchtime measured by years I lie awake
elbowed on the Atreidae's roof dogwise to mark
the grand processionals of all the stars of night
burdened with winter and again with heat for men,
dynasties in their shining blazoned on the air,
these stars, upon their wane and when the rest arise.
{RICHMOND LATTIMORE}

Of the gods I ask deliverance from this toil, from my year-long
watch, in which, lying at the house of the Atridae on my arms,
dog-fashion, I have become familiar with the assembly of the stars
of night, and those bright potentates conspicuous in the sky who
bring winter and summer to man.
{EDUARD FRAENKEL}

I've lain here a year,
crouching like a dog on one elbow,
and begged the gods to end my watch.

I've watched the stars. I know their comings
and goings, the bringers of winter and the bringers
of summer. The stars burn with power,
and rule their empty spaces like kings.
{ROBERT LOWELL}

Dear gods, set me free from all the pain,
from the watch I keep, one whole year awake . . .
propped on my arms, crouched on the roofs of Atreus like a god.

     I know the stars by heart,
the armies of the night, and there in the lead
the ones that bring us snow or the crops of summer,
bring us all we have—
our great blazing kings of the sky,
I know them, when they rise and when they fall . . .
{ROBERT FAGLES}

No end to it all, though all year I've muttered
my pleas to the gods for a long groped for end.
Wish it were over, this waiting, this watching,
twelve weary months, night in and night out,
crouching and peering, head down like a bloodhound,
paws propping muzzle, up here on the palace,
the palace belonging the bloodclan of Atreus—
Agamemnon, Menelaus, bloodkin, our clanchiefs.

I've been so long staring I know the stars backwards, the
chiefs of the star-clans, king-stars, controllers,
those that dispense us the coldsnaps and dogdays.
I've had a whole year's worth so I ought to know.
{TONY HARRISON}

I beg the gods; release me from these sufferings,
This year-long watch that I have lain
Huddled upon the house of Atreus' sons, just like a dog.
I've come to know the mass of stars assembled in the night
And those bright overlords, who bring to mortal men
Winter and summer—stars that shine clear in the sky
Both when they set and when they rise.
{MICHAEL EWANS}

Of these versions, that by Robert Potter is from the earliest English translation of the plays of Aeschylus, first published in 1777. Gilbert Murray was a scholar, whose versions of a number of Euripides' tragedies helped to bring Greek tragedy to the attention of London theater audiences at the beginning of this century. Louis MacNeice is the Irish poet, associated closely with W. H. Auden, and his translation was published in the thirties. Richmond Lattimore was a poet, and coeditor of one of the major postwar series of translations of Greek tragedy, published by the University of Chicago Press. Eduard Fraenkel was a scholar, who published (in 1950) an extensive edition of *Agamemnon,* which included a prose translation alongside the Greek text. Robert Lowell is the American poet, who wrote his version of this play in the early sixties. Robert Fagles' translation is published in Penguin Classics, the second of the major postwar series of translations of Greek plays; in the later seventies it replaced an earlier version by Philip Vellacott. Tony Harrison is an English poet, who wrote this version of Aeschylus' *Oresteia* for a production (in masks) by the National Theatre which opened in London in late 1981, and transferred to the Greek theater at Epidarus in the following year. Michael Ewans is a theater studies scholar who develops the sound of his close translations in workshops with actors, as one part of his practical research into the performance of the scripts.

The extracts given here are clearly too short for significant critical analysis, and represent only a selection, with a bias toward the later twentieth century; but they do provide an indication of variety, and of the problems facing translators. These will often vary according to whether the author is directing attention predominantly to a readership or to a live audience. At one end of the spectrum, a translation may be produced as an aid to close study of the original text, as was the case with Fraenkel. In versions of this kind the receiving language may risk some distortion in providing an equivalent of the patterns and distinctions of the original. On the other hand, as is the case with Harrison, a contemporary mode may be demanded for modern theatrical resources and conditions which will result in a relatively free version, or perhaps an adaptation.

The history of adaptation is of considerable importance in relation to some theatrical cultures. In France, Jean Racine adapted tragedies by Euripides for his *Iphigénie* and *Phédre* in the seventeenth century; and in Germany Goethe, toward the end of the eighteenth century, turned to another play by Euripides for his *Iphigenie auf Tauris*. In the twentieth century both cultures have again shown a strong interest in Greek tragedy, with the plays of Cocteau (*La Machine Infernale,* drawing on the Oedipus legend), Giraudoux (*Electre*), Anouilh (*Antigone*), and Sartre (*Les Mouches, Les Troyennes*) in French; and those of Hofmannsthal (notably *Electra*) and the tetralogy on the house of Atreus by Hauptmann in German. In the United States a major impact was achieved by Eugene O'Neill with *Mourning Becomes Electra,* his adaptation of Aeschylus' *Oresteia*. In the British theater, the influence firstly of the Roman tragedian Seneca on Elizabethan tragedy and then that of Molière on the later restoration comedy have tended to stifle direct interest in Greek models, until the strong contemporary revival of Greek tragedies on radio and television, as well as on the stage.

The comments of those who adapt offer an interesting insight into the problems of translation. Looking back to the seventeenth century, for Racine Euripides was the most dominant of a number of sources, which he is at pains to acknowledge in his prefaces. In the preface he published to *Iphigénie,* he was conscious that he had distanced himself a little from "the economy and the plot of Euripides. But in so far as the passions are concerned, I have made every effort to follow him exactly." For *Phèdre,* his acknowledgment was couched in similar terms:

> Here once again is a tragedy whose subject has been taken from Euripides. Although I have followed a different path from that author in the conduct of the action, I have not failed to enrich my play with everything that struck me as most brilliant in his.

The emphasis here on the passions, and on what is "brilliant" or "striking" (*éclatant*) suggests a consistent concern for certain qualities of the original which may be distinguished from the actual language and construction of the play. This attitude is reflected in the modern period by comments from two further adapters, who develop their ideas in terms that are bound to be more familiar. The first passage is taken from observations made by Jean-Paul Sartre on his adaptation of Euripides' *Trojan Women,* performed and published in the mid-sixties; the second is by David Rudkin, in the foreword to his version of Euripides' *Hippolytus,* first performed by the Royal Shakespeare Company in Britain in 1978.

> There was an implicit rapport between Euripides and the audience for which he was writing. It is something which we can see but not share. Since this relationship was implicit, a translation cannot reproduce it. It was therefore necessary to adapt the play.
>
> {JEAN-PAUL SARTRE}

The reader—and spectator—may wish to know the relationship between this text and the original. I have rendered, line by line, not an abstract linguistic equivalent of the Greek, but what I understand its living significances to be. In matters of theology and myth (geography too), to us Greek references are practically meaningless. On the page, explanatory foot-notes can be provided. In the theater, we must know, in the drama's vital presence, what is actually being said. So must the actor. To achieve this, an interpretative commitment must be risked; an interpretation, though defined and governed by the letter of the text. A translation of a play is like a production of that play: it represents a moral response to it.

The Greek dramatists are important. In the theater, I want to encounter what they are saying to me, not what they once said to someone else. Paradoxically, we might only ever approach the "original experience" of Athenian tragedy by first expunging from it every element we think of as "Greek". Euripides' audience weren't watching a "Greek" play. They were watching a play of their own. So must we be.

{DAVID RUDKIN}

The promise of adapters is that the demands posed by theatrical performance will inevitably create a new, living theatrical work; but it may be equally possible that this script itself, once published, will be deprived of some of the vitality that performance brought to it. So we find that translations which are principally intended for a reading public will often record the particular details of the original without any marked attempt to adapt them. This is presumably because the distance of a translated work, in both time and language in the case of Greek drama, can be as important to some readers as its vitality across two cultures. Put simply, people may want to know "what was there" as much as they would like to experience "how it felt." And in some cases the adapters themselves, unless they know the original language, will have had to rely on translations. Seen from this perspective, there is no real contradiction between adaptation and translation: they simply serve different purposes.

The specific problems faced by translators of Greek tragedy occur largely in two areas, those of language and meter. Greek drama is composed, as was mentioned above ("The Writer" and "Choral Song and Choral Action") of spoken or chanted delivery and song, but the music and dance steps are missing. The problem is complicated by the fact that ancient Greek was an inflected language (spoken by pitch rather than stress), and so the metrical rhythm that can be seen in the text was only one of several influences affecting sound. But translators of tragedy invariably work by finding some equivalent rather than by discarding verse altogether; and a traditional solution has been to equate the spoken parts of the plays with the five-stress rhythm of English blank verse, since this is familiar to the ear from Elizabethan drama. Rhyme is not a feature of Greek drama, although it has appeared in some translations and adaptations (e.g., Murray, above). The complexity of rhythm in song has generally defeated the search for equivalents, and translators usually concentrate on language and clarity, since choral song is notoriously difficult to understand. But any rhythm translators into English do adopt will be based, however variably, on stress; and choral passages are usually marked out in translation by the simple expedient of shorter lines, largely a reflection of the way they are presented in editions of the original text.

The problems of language are immensely complex, and are resolved individually, as can be seen in the variety of even the small number of selections I have given from translations of *Agamemnon*. Typical obstacles for the close translator are limitations in the choice of verbal equivalents, lack of correspondence in expression between ancient Greek and English, and a discrepancy in the order of emphasis or construction in both languages. The original script obviously represents decisions by the particular author, and the pattern of these decisions may also vary over his lifetime, and from play to play. So there can never be "a model" for translating one of the dramatists, though there are separate arguments in favor of a diversity of translators (as in the Chicago series) or for one translator covering a body of work by one or more authors (as has regularly been the case in Penguin Classics).

Criticisms of translations will generally refer to "style," or, on occasion, to points of accuracy. Despite the apparently fault-finding quality of the second count, it is probably more valuable, since "style" is clearly close to taste and is a subject on which it is notably difficult to come to any firm agreement. In reviewing critical reactions to translations, it is probably fair to say that translators have generally succeeded less, and their translations been less long-lived or popular, when they have approached their work with a fixed sense of an established convention in poetry (or, perhaps worse, of an established convention in translation). The simple reason for this is that Greek drama obviously reaches behind any existing conventions in the reader's understanding to a historically remote period that a direct association with any period in the recent past is almost bound to disrupt. Those who write adaptations are perhaps particularly conscious of this (e.g., Rudkin), and Harrison came up with an interesting solution by pitching his version behind the main body of English literature into what he described as "ghostly Anglo-Saxon rhythms." The choices of an adapter will be open to critical reaction; but the moral they pose for translators is reasonably clear.

The comedies of Aristophanes have been far less widely adopted into modern languages and cultures than Greek tragedy, and the difficulties they offer for translators are complicated in particular by their insistent topicality, in jokes, subject matter, and allusions to contemporary figures. The sexual and excremental humor of Aristophanes did not encourage modern European versions, and where they existed they tended to be "bowdlerized" or censored. The sixties in the United States proved free from this inhibition, and the most vigorous translations probably date from that time. Translators generally discard verse forms for comedy, though British translators have a tendency to suggest Victorian or older "tunes" as a background accompaniment to some of Aristophanes' songs, which seems a strange association, and one which is rapidly losing whatever point it had. The range of existing translations is far less wide than that for many tragedies, but their diversity seems at least as great. Topical references (to personalities, events) and puns are two obvious problems in connection with laughter; and both are involved in the comprehensive difficulty of translating an intricate cultural context for the plays—involving political, artistic, legal, social, and religious institutions and assumptions—into a form which will carry both humor and conviction across to a modern audience.

The scale of some of these problems has seen criticism generally draw back from translations of Aristophanes, probably because it is felt that neither accuracy nor consistency of "style" is likely to be as significant as adroitness (or the lack of it) in re-creating humor. In other words, a translation is either "funny" or not. But this reaction may not be enough: Aristophanic comedy was certainly meant to make people laugh, but there is more to it than being simply funny. There would seem to be quite a strong case now for a distinction between freehanded versions and translations which permit close access without adaptation. One approach to the problem, adopted in the Penguin Classics series, is to append historical notes to a relatively close translation, and for certain purposes this is helpful. Probably the main obstacle to the successful translation of Aristophanes is, in fact, the lack of stimulating demand from the theater or other media. With the exception of *Lysistrata,* and on occasions *Frogs,* and apart from regular productions by the Greek National Theatre, there have been relatively few performances of Aristophanes' comedies, and few directly commissioned scripts. This has almost certainly dictated a lack of initiative.

Versions of some of the Greek plays exist on film, and the themes of the plays have had a far wider impact than their relatively direct reproductions in any one of the available contemporary media. This cultural vitality can only be assured by some continuing provision for study of the original language, which is most effective when it is linked to close attention to the originals as theatrical scripts. For readers or for audiences, renewed translation or adaptation will secure access to a body of work that has repeatedly demonstrated its appeal, most notably and widely in the twentieth century, and particularly in the period since 1945.

APPENDIX

Chronology of the Surviving Plays

The known dates are those of production. The positioning of other plays remains uncertain. (Ae.) = Aeschylus; (S.) = Sophocles; (E.) = Euripides; (Ar.) = Aristophanes.

---

472 B.C.   *The Persians* (Ae.)

467 B.C.   *Seven against Thebes* (Ae.)

463 B.C.   *The Suppliant Maidens* (Ae.)

458 B.C.   *Agamemnon, The Libation Bearers, The Eumenides* (the *Oresteia* trilogy) (Ae.)

?   *Ajax* (S.)

?   *Antigone* (S.)

438 B.C.   *Alcestis* (E.)

?   *The Women of Trachis* (S.)

431 B.C.   *The Medea* (E.)

?   *Oedipus the King* (S.)

?   *The Heracleidae* (E.)

428 B.C.   *Hippolytus* (E.)

?   *Andromache* (E.)

425 B.C.   *Acharnians* (Ar.)

424 B.C.   *Knights* (Ar.)

423 B.C.   *Clouds* (Ar.)

?	*The Suppliant Women* (E.)
?	*Hecuba* (E.)
422 B.C.	*Wasps* (Ar.)
421 B.C.	*Peace* (Ar.)
?	*Electra* (E.)
?	*Heracles* (E.)
415 B.C.	*The Trojan Women* (E.)
414 B.C.	*Birds* (Ar.)
?	*Iphigenia in Tauris* (E.)
?	*Ion* (E.)
412 B.C.	*Helen* (E.)
411 B.C.	*Lysistrata* (Ar.); *Women at the Thesmophoria* (Ar.)
?	*Electra* (S.)
?	*The Phoenician Women* (E.)
?	*The Cyclops* (E.)
409 B.C.	*Philoctetes* (S.)
408 B.C.	*Orestes* (E.)
405 B.C.	*Frogs* (Ar.)
?	*The Bacchae* (E.); *Iphigenia in Aulis* (E.)
401 B.C.	*Oedipus at Colonus* (S.)
391 B.C.	*Women in Assembly* (Ar.)
388 B.C.	*Wealth* (Ar.)

Prometheus Bound, formerly attributed to Aeschylus, is of unknown authorship and date, as is *Rhesus,* attributed to Euripides.

The productions of *Lysistrata* and *Women at the Thesmophoria* in 411 B.C. will presumably have been at different festivals (Lenaea and City Dionysia).

All the plays of Aristophanes are comedies. *Cyclops* by Euripides is a satyr play, and his *Alcestis* is a play composed to take the place of a satyr play. The rest are tragedies.

GLOSSARY

agora	public meeting place, market, and sanctuary
akropolis	citadel
archon	magistrate
auletes	pipe player
bema	speaking platform
choregos/-oi	citizen(s) appointed to pay for the presentation of a choros
choros/-oi	singing and dancing group(s) of performers
didaskalos	(teacher), trainer, playwright/composer
drama	(action), a play
ekklesia	political assembly of citizens
ekkuklema	rolling platform
hypokrites	actor
kothornos/-oi	soft boot(s)
mechane	(machine), crane
orchestra	dancing floor
poietes	(maker), poet, playwright
prosopon/-a	mask(s)
prosopopoios/-oi	mask maker(s)
skene	(tent), scene building
theatron	theater, auditorium

BIBLIOGRAPHY

The bibliography is of works in English, although one or two of the books quote in Greek, without translation. The list is extremely selective, and is intended simply as a guide to some further reading.

Source Materials and Photographs

The abbreviations are those given in the text to identify illustrations.

E. Csapo and W. L. Slater. *The Context of Ancient Drama.* Ann Arbor, 1994.

HGRT = Bieber, M. *The History of the Greek and Roman Theater,* 2d ed. Princeton, 1961.

DTC = Pickard-Cambridge, A. W. *Dithyramb, Tragedy, and Comedy,* 2d ed. (revised by T. B. L. Webster). Oxford, 1962.

DFA = Pickard-Cambridge, A. W. *The Dramatic Festivals of Athens,* 2d ed. (revised by J. Gould and D. M. Lewis), reissued with a supplement. Oxford, 1988.

Pickard-Cambridge, A. W. *The Theatre of Dionysus at Athens.* Oxford, 1946.

IGD = Trendall, A. D., and T. B. L. Webster. *Illustrations of Greek Drama.* London, 1971.

Webster, T. B. L. *Greek Theatre Production,* 2d ed. London, 1970.

General Surveys

Arnott, P. D. *Public Performance in the Greek Theatre.* London, 1989.

Dover, K. J. *Aristophanic Comedy.* Berkeley and L. A., 1972.

Flickinger, R. C. *The Greek Theater and Its Drama,* 4th ed. Chicago, 1936.

Lesky, A. *Greek Tragedy,* 3d ed. London, 1978.

Norwood, G. *Greek Comedy.* London, 1931.

Reckford, K. J. *Aristophanes' Old and New Comedy,* vol. 1. Chapel Hill, 1987.

Rehm, R. *Greek Tragic Theatre.* London, 1994.

Russo, C. F. *Aristophanes, an Author for the Stage.* London and New York, 1994.

Vickers, B. *Towards Greek Tragedy.* London, 1973.

Wiles, D. *Greek Theatre Performance: An Introduction.* Cambridge, 2000.

N.B. For the later comic writer Menander, the translation of plays and fragments in the Penguin Classics series is up-to-date, and includes a short bibliography.

Greek Drama

Useful, short general surveys of Greek drama in the wider context of the surviving literature: K. J. Dover (ed.), *Ancient Greek Literature,* Oxford, 1981; and J. de Romilly, *A Short History of Greek Literature,* Chicago, 1985. Concise surveys of tragedy and comedy, including a catalogue-type discussion of the surviving plays: the books by Lesky and Dover (listed above, under "General Surveys").

The dramatic texts are the subject of section I of the translated sources in Csapo and Slater, *The Context of Ancient Drama* (listed above, under "Sources"). Translations of some of the fragments of plays by Aeschylus are available in M. Ewans, *Aeschylus: Suppliants and Other Dramas,* London and New York, 1996; of fragments of plays by Sophocles in H. Lloyd-Jones, *Sophocles: Fragments,* Cambridge, Mass., 1996; and of Euripides in C. Collard, M. J. Cropp, and K. H. Lee, *Euripides: Selected Fragmentary Plays Vol. I,* Warminster, 1995; and C. Collard, M. J. Cropp and J. Gibert (eds.), *Euripides: Selected Fragmentary Plays Vol. II,* Oxford, 2004. For comic playwrights other than Aristophanes: J. Wilkins and D. Harvey (eds.), *The Rivals of Aristophanes,* London, 2000. For satyric drama: D. F. Sutton, *The Greek Satyr-Play,* Meisenheim, 1980; and the introduction by R. Seaford to his edition of Euripides' *Cyclops,* Oxford, 1984.

The Organization of the Festivals

The standard work in English is the second edition of Pickard-Cambridge, *The Dramatic Festivals of Athens* (listed above, under "Sources"), reissued with a supplement in 1988. But this may now be read alongside the discussion and presentation of translated sources in section IIIA of Csapo and Slater, *The Context of Ancient Drama* (above, "Sources"). A more concise summary of the country and city festivals of Dionysus is given by H. W. Parke, *Festivals of the Athenians,* London, 1977 (country, 100–103; Lenaea, 104–6; City Dionysia, 125–36). On the connection between Dionysus and drama in the festivals at Athens: P. E. Easterling, "A Show for Dionysus," a chapter in her edited volume, *The Cambridge Companion to Greek Tragedy,* Cambridge, 1997. P. Wilson, *The Athenian Institution of the Khoregia,* Cambridge, 2000, is a broad-ranging and detailed study. K. McLeish, *The Theatre of Aristophanes,* London, 1980, has some helpful comments on preparations in his second chapter, "The Practical Playwright." On tragedy outside Athens: O. Taplin, "Spreading the Word through Performance," a chapter in S. Goldhill and R. Osborne (eds.), *Performance Culture and Athenian Democracy,* Cambridge, 1999.

Lesser Dramatic Performances at Athens

There are several major studies of the history of puppetry that include a section on antiquity; the most recent is H. Jurkowski, *A History of European Puppetry Volume One: From Its Origins to the End of the Nineteenth Century,* Dyfed, 1996. M. Byrom, *The Puppet Theatre in Antiquity,* Bicester, 1996, is an interesting pamphlet. The fragments of the mimes of Sophron, with Greek text and translation, can be found in J. Rusten and I. C. Cunningham (eds.), *Theophrastus: Characters, Herodas: Mimes, Sophron and Other Mime Fragments,* Cambridge, Mass., 2002. The fragments are translated, with an introduction on Sophron and the mimes, by J. H. Hordern, *Sophron's Mimes,* Oxford, 2004. There is an extended discussion of the performance in Xenophon's *Symposium* in its context of "Sympotic Space" in D. Wiles, *A Short History of Western Performance Space,* Cambridge, 2003. There are several translations of Xenophon's *Symposium* available: e.g., R. C. Bartlett (ed.), *Xenophon: The Shorter Socratic Writings: Apology of Socrates to the Jury, Oeconomicus, and Symposium,* Ithaca, 1996. H. Denard has written a survey of the forms of performance in classical antiquity other than tragedy, comedy and satyr play: "Lost Theatre and Performance Traditions in Greece and Italy," a chapter in M. Walton and M. McDonald (eds.), *The Cambridge Companion to Greek and Roman Theatre,* Cambridge, 2007.

The Writer

The historical background to the skills required of the Athenian tragedians is the subject of the Sather Lectures by J. Herington, *Poetry into Drama: Early Tragedy and the Greek Poetic Tradition,* Berkeley and L.A., 1985. On the role and tasks of the *choregos:* Part 1.2 in Wilson (above, ". . . Festivals").

The Theater

The standard work in English on the archaeological remains of the principal festival site is still Pickard-Cambridge, *The Theatre of Dionysus at Athens* (above, "Sources"). A more recent interpretation of the ruins can be found in J. Travlos, *A Pictorial Dictionary of Athens,* London, 1971. C. W. Dearden, *The Stage of Aristophanes,* London, 1976, is a specialized study of the problems relating to comedy. D. Wiles, *Tragedy in Athens,* Cambridge, 1997, reviews the current debate on the construction and shape of the playing space incisively in his second chapter, "The Theatre of Dionysus." D. Mastronarde, "Actors on High: The Skene Roof, the Crane, and the Gods in Attic Drama," *Classical Antiquity* 9.2 (1990), 248–94, is valuable on the *mechane.*

Scenography

The best treatments of the circumstances surrounding the invention of scenography are to be found in surveys of Greek art: for example, M. Robertson, *A History of Greek Art,* Cambridge, 1981 (see index under Agatharchos, reputedly the originator of the art). Though written some four centuries after the plays, *On Architecture* by Vitruvius is the earliest surviving treatise of its kind. There is a parallel Latin/English text in the Loeb Classical Library: the observations on Agatharchos come at the beginning of book 7. A conclusion in favor of a limited number of standard sets is offered by N. C. Hourmouziades, *Production and Imagination in Euripides,* Athens, 1965. If the front of the wooden *skene* was constructed of panels, then these might be used for the painting of settings, or removed to create additional doors or openings: J.-C. Moretti, "The Theater of the Sanctuary of Dionysus Eleuthereus in Late Fifth-Century Athens," a chapter in M. Cropp, K. Lee, and D. Sansone (eds.), *Euripides and Tragic Theatre in the Late Fifth Century,* Champaign, Ill., 2000; also *Illinois Classical Studies* xxiv–xxv (1999–2000).

Masks, Costume, and Properties

A good range of pictures for the fifth century is available in Pickard-Cambridge, *DFA* and *DTC;* and Bieber, *HGRT* (listed above, "Sources"). Webster in *Greek Theatre Production* (above, "Sources") extends his discussion into greater detail for the later theater of Menander. O. Taplin, *Greek Tragedy in Action,* London, 1978, gives chap. 6, "Objects and Tokens," to properties. I have reviewed the use of costume and properties in "A Material World: Costume, Properties and Scenic Effects," a chapter in M. Walton and M. McDonald (eds.), *The Cambridge Companion to Greek and Roman Theatre,* Cambridge, 2007. Wiles, *Greek Theatre Performance* (above, "General Surveys") considers the mask in the light of contemporary thinking and practice in his chapter "The Performer." The most comprehensive discussion of any aspect is L. M. Stone, *Costume in Aristophanic Poetry,* New York, 1981.

Chorus

A selection of the varieties of nondramatic choral song is conveniently presented in translation in R. Lattimore, *Greek Lyric Poetry,* Chicago, 1960. The same author's translation of the choral songs of Pindar (a near-contemporary of Aeschylus) composed for victors in the athletic games of Greece is also recommended. Evidence on training and preparation is collected in Pickard-Cambridge, *DFA.* Detailed speculations on the choral origins of both tragedy and comedy are to be found in Pickard-Cambridge, *DTC,* and the sources are translated and presented in section II of Csapo and Slater, *The Context of Ancient Drama* (above, "Sources"). I have discussed the early evidence for the *choros,* and reviewed the evidence for both music and dancing, in the second chapter of *The Theatricality of Greek Tragedy: Playing Space and Chorus,* Chicago, 2006. There is an interesting collection of essays in H. Golder and S. Scully (eds.), *The Chorus in Greek Tragedy and Culture, One and Two;* also *Arion,* Third Series 3.1 and 4.1 (1995 and 1996).

Actors

Pickard-Cambridge, *DFA,* chap. 3, contains most of the ancient evidence, and a scheme for the distribution of roles between performers. The evidence linking Euaion and Sophocles is discussed by T. B. L. Webster, *Potter and Painter in Classical Athens,* London, 1972; and presented in the introduction, "Theatre Art and Its Patrons," to Trendall and Webster, *IGD* (above, "Sources"). Some conclusions about acting technique can be drawn from Taplin (above, under "Masks . . ."); and McLeish (above, under ". . . Festivals"). P. Easterling and E. Hall (eds.), *Greek and Roman Actors: Aspects of an Ancient Profession,* Cambridge, 2002, is a wide-ranging collection of essays on the art, profession and idea of the actor.

Reading Texts as Scripts

There are useful observations on the principles of costuming, and the distinctions achieved by costume, in the introduction by S. D. Olson (ed.), *Aristophanes: Acharnians,* Oxford, 2002. J. P. Poe, "Multiplicity, Discontinuity, and Visual Meaning in Aristophanic Comedy," *Rheinische Museum* 14.3 (2000), 256–95, provides indicative lists of properties, and subjects their use in Aristophanes to a close analysis. I discuss the relationship of leading characters to the chorus, both in tragedy and comedy, at greater length in *The Theatricality of Greek Tragedy* (above, "Chorus").

The Playing Space

The best summary description is in Webster, *Greek Theatre Production* (above, "Sources"). On the problem of doors in the *skene*, see my comments and the reference to Moretti above, under "Scenography." R. Rehm, *The Play of Space: Spatial Transformation in Greek Tragedy*, Princeton, 2002, is an expansive study of tragic scripts that is rooted in the playing space. Wiles in *Tragedy in Athens* (above, "Theater") offers a structural and semiotic interpretation of the playing space in Greek cultural space. I have concentrated on how tragic scripts were realized in the open ground of the playing space in the first chapter of *The Theatricality of Greek Tragedy* (above, "Chorus").

The Audience

Whether women freely attended performances in the theater is sharply debated: S. Goldhill, "The Audience of Athenian Tragedy," a chapter in Easterling, *The Cambridge Companion to Greek Tragedy* (above, ". . . Festivals") presents a summary of arguments. E. Hall, "The Sociology of Athenian Tragedy," another chapter in the same volume, introduces attitudes to gender and class; perhaps the most informative study in the relationship between the Athenian audience and its theater remains V. Ehrenberg, *The People of Aristophanes*, 2d ed., Oxford, 1951. H. P. Foley (ed.), *Reflections of Women in Antiquity*, New York, 1981, examines attitudes surrounding women characters in the theater, and Foley's *Female Acts*, Princeton, 2003, offers sophisticated gender criticism. Section IIIAiib in Csapo and Slater, *The Context of Ancient Drama* (above, "Sources") reviews the ancient evidence on judges of the dramatic competitions, while section IVBi discusses and presents translated sources relating to the fifth-century audience. Aspects of social history are conveniently grouped in a publication by the Joint Association of Classical Teachers, *The World of Athens,* Cambridge, 1984. Details and diagrams of the political assembly place are given in Travlos (above, "The Theater") under "Pnyx." The audience and the community feature prominently in the studies collected by J. J. Winckler and F. I. Zeitlin (eds.), *Nothing To Do With Dionysos?: Athenian Drama in Its Social Context,* Princeton, 1990.

Delivery

The best approach to the problem of "delivery" in the Athenian theater is to read speeches from the law courts and political assembly from a comparable period: one available selection is *Greek Political Oratory* in the Penguin Classics series. Highly sophisticated, contemporary speech composition on a theme close to tragedy is represented by Gorgias' *Encomium of Helen,* translated with an introduction by D. M. McDowell, Bristol, 1982. Facets of public speaking are considered in an essay collection by I. Worthington (ed.), *Persuasion: Greek Rhetoric in Action,* London and New York, 1993. R. G. A. Buxton, *Persuasion in Greek Tragedy: A Study of Peitho,* Cambridge, 1982, is useful in relation to this and the previous topic, as is S. Halliwell, "Between Public and Private: Tragedy and Athenian Experience of Rhetoric," a chapter in C. Pelling (ed.), *Greek Tragedy and the Historian,* New York, 1997.

Distance and Physical Action

The action of tragedy is the subject of Taplin's book (above, "Masks . . ."); and comedy in performance is the subject of the book by McLeish (above, ". . . Festivals"). D. Seale, *Vision and Stagecraft in Sophocles,* London, 1982; and M. Halleran, *Stagecraft in Euripides,* London, 1984, should also be considered. M. Kaimio, *Physical Contact in Greek Tragedy,* Helsinki, 1988, is a valuable study. I have explored evidence for the disposition of performers in the playing space in the first chapter of *The Theatricality of Greek Tragedy* (above, "Chorus").

Choral Song and Choral Action

Discussions of the dramatic chorus have usually been confined to language: for example, R. W. B. Burton, *The Chorus in Sophocles' Tragedies,* Oxford, 1980; to which the different approach of C. P. Gardiner, *The Sophoclean Chorus,* Iowa, 1987, can be compared. I review other approaches to the tragic chorus, to its song and its dancing, in the second chapter of *The Theatricality of Greek Tragedy* (above, "Chorus"). P. Wilson, "The *aulos* in Athens," a chapter in Goldhill and Osborne, *Performance Culture and Athenian Democracy* (above, ". . . Festivals"), considers the function and significance of the *auletes.* I examine aspects of the disposition of the chorus with the actors, notably in sequences of song and dancing, in the first chapter of *The Theatricality of Greek Tragedy.* Rehm in the second chapter of *The Play of Space* (above, "The Playing Space") offers an intriguing interpretation of the first appearance of the chorus in Aeschylus' *Eumenides.* An extended analysis of the complex forms, including the *parabasis,* of Aristophanes' comedies is available in Pickard-Cambridge, *DTC,* in a discussion which contains some suggestions on presentation, while T. K. Hubbard, *The Mask of Comedy: Aristophanes and the Intertextual Parabasis,* Ithaca, 1991, adds a critical voice to considerations of comic form.

Parody

All books on Aristophanes will make some reference to parody. The fragments of Euripides' *Telephos* are available in translation and with a commentary in Collard, Cropp, and Lee, *Euripides: Selected Fragmentary Plays Vol. 1* (above "Greek Drama"). An interesting comparison of three different tragic treatments of the same myth (*Philoctetes*) in an order that we can determine (Aeschylus—?, Euripides—431 B.C., and Sophocles—409 B.C.) survives from the Roman imperial period, and is translated in D. A. Russell and M. Winterbottom, *Ancient Literary Criticism,* Oxford, 1972, chap. 12A. B. Knox, *Word and Action: Essays on the Ancient Greek Theatre,* Baltimore, 1979, has a valuable essay in chap. 19, "Euripidean comedy."

For parody as it affects women in an important play for the subject, see F. R. Zeitlin, "Travesties of Gender and Genre in Aristophanes' *Thesmophoriazousae*," another essay in the collection edited by Foley (above, "The Audience"). Parody engages with the larger idea of metatheatre: N. Slater, *Spectator Politics: Metatheatre and Performance in Aristophanes,* Philadelphia, 2002.

Translation and Adaptation

One of the best modern (though not now contemporary) reviews of translation is by P. Green, *Essays in Antiquity,* London, 1960, chap. 9, "Some Versions of Aeschylus," which has a commentary on a number of the translations here. Further commentary on the translation by MacNeice (from Michael Sidnell) and the version by Tony Harrison (from R. B. Parker) is available in M. Cropp, E. Fantham, S. E. Scully (eds.), *Greek Tragedy and Its Legacy: Essays Presented to D. J. Conacher,* Calgary, 1986. L. Hardwick, *Translating Words, Translating Cultures,* London, 2000, contains valuable insights, including a critical assessment of Harrison's film poem *Prometheus* of 1998, and Hardwick provides an ampler bibliography in her *Reception Studies,* Oxford, 2003. Major works exist by G. Steiner, on translation (*After Babel: Aspects of Language and Translation History,* London, 1975); and on "versions," or adaptation and influence (*Antigones,* Oxford, 1984). J. R. Mackinnon, *Greek Tragedy into Film,* London, 1986, explores adaptation into one contemporary medium. The literature on translation is extensive, but some acute perceptions are expressed in particular by W. Benjamin, "The Task of the Translator," in *Illuminations,* London, 1970, a volume of his essays edited by H. Arendt. The fragments of Sophocles' *The Searching Satyrs* provided the inspiration for Tony Harrison's playscript *The Trackers of Oxyrhynchus,* London, 1991.

The critical study of post-classical and modern production is expanding: J. M. Walton, *Living Greek Theatre: A Handbook of Classical Performance and Modern Production,* London, 1988, and M. McDonald, *Ancient Sun Modern Light: Greek Drama on the Modern Stage,* New York, 1992, with the essays in P. E. Easterling (ed.), *The Cambridge Companion to Greek Tragedy* (above, ". . . Festivals"), Part III: Reception. Conferences and published studies on aspects of the post-classical production of individual plays arise from the work of The Archive of Performances of Greek and Roman Drama: E. Hall, F. Macintosh and O. Taplin (eds.), *Medea in Performance 1500–2000*, Oxford, 2000. The online journal *Didaskalia* publishes news and reviews of translations, adaptations and productions.

Translations

The complete Greek tragedies are published by the University of Chicago Press, and one volume of the series, *Euripides II*, includes a translation of Euripides' satyr play, *Cyclops*. A complete series of translations of Greek tragedy and of the comedies of Aristophanes is available in Penguin Classics and from Methuen.

Other translations of individual plays, or groups of plays, are available from a number of sources, and parallel Greek/English texts are published in the Loeb Classical Library (Heinemann), and by Aris and Phillips.

The translated plays and fragments of Menander are available in Penguin Classics.

PLATE 1. Performer and chorus. Antikenmuseum Basel und Sammlung Ludwig, Inv. BS 415: Attic red-figured column *krater*, about 480 B.C.: photo Claire Niggli.

PLATE 3. Detail, lower panel: Prometheus and satyrs. Ashmolean Museum, Oxford, 1937.983: Attic red-figured *kalyx krater*, by the Dinos Painter, about 425–420 B.C.

PLATE 2. Side A: Performers dressing (also known as "Actors dressing"). H. L. Pierce Fund, courtesy Museum of Fine Arts, Boston, 98.883: Attic red-figured *pelike*, by the Painter of the Boston Phiale, about 430 B.C.: h. 24.1 cm., diam. 18 cm.

PLATE 4. *Aulos* player flanked by performers dressed as cocks. Collection of the J. Paul Getty Museum, Malibu, California, 82.AE.83: Attic red-figured *kalyx krater,* unknown artist, after 415 B.C. Terra-cotta: h. 19 cm., diam. 23.2 cm.

PLATE 5. Illustration of Euripides' *Andromeda*. Staatliche Museen zu Berlin, Antiken-sammlung, V.I.3237: Attic red-figured *kalyx krater,* about 400 B.C.

PLATE 6. Illustration of Euripides' *Antiope*. Antikenmuseum Berlin, Staatliche Museen preussischer Kulturbesitz, F3296: Sicilian red-figured *kalyx krater*, by the Dirce Painter, about 380 B.C.: photo Isolde Luckert.

PLATE 7. A female acrobat on a wheel turned by a masked comic performer. Ashmolean Museum, Oxford, 1945.43: Paestan red-figured *skyphos*, about 350–325 B.C.

COMMENTARY

on the PLATES

PLATE 1. An Athenian wine-mixing bowl (*krater*) from the period of the Persian Wars, just before the earliest surviving plays. The six singing and dancing figures wear diadems and sleeveless patterned jackets. The similarity of the faces, and the pronounced jaw line, strongly suggest masks. The different positions of the arms may indicate a sweeping gesture of obeisance to the figure wrapped in a cloak, who rises behind a stepped and adorned altar or tomb. The number of the dancers is half that of the early tragic chorus.

PLATE 2. An Athenian jug (*pelike*), from the period of Euripides' *Medea* and *Hippolytus*. Two members of a (tragic) chorus of women, identified as such from the similarity of their masks. The performer on the right has bound his hair, in preparation for putting on his mask, and both wear (soft) boots with curved toes. The second performer is fully costumed and masked, and hands a final garment to the first, with a "theatrical" gesture. The illustration comes from the Phiale Painter, who shows a strong interest in the theater in his works.

PLATE 3. The lower panel of a painting on an Athenian wine-mixing bowl. One of a series of pictures which seem to illustrate a lost satyr play by Aeschylus, composed a generation before, in which Prometheus brought fire to men in fennel stalks, helped or hindered by satyrs. These satyrs bear no traces of theatrical costume, but the gestures and steps are almost certainly those of performers. It is likely that more than one moment of a dance is shown here—aspects of a sequence—which illustrates the problems surrounding the reconstruction of theatrical dance.

PLATE 4. An Athenian wine-mixing bowl from the later fifth century. A rare illustration of comedy from this period, with two performers as fighting cocks, on either side of a pipe player. They are wearing decorated body stockings, and loincloths to which the tail and erect *phallos* are fixed, in addition to wings, masks, and spurs. They may be members of a comic chorus, or paired comic performers in conflict. The presence of the pipe player and their movements suggest they are dancing. The chorus of Aristophanes' *Birds* was of wild birds, but the picture provides us with a model.

PLATE 5. An Athenian wine-mixing bowl, from the end of the fifth century. The named figure of Andromeda stands with her arms fastened to rocks, in a decorated sleeved costume, and wearing an oriental headdress, as does Kepheus, her father, to her right. To her other side stands Perseus, her rescuer. Above Kepheus is Hermes, the guiding god, and above Perseus the goddess Aphrodite (not fully shown), holding a wreath over his head. The boxes would contain offerings, and the painter has shown leaves and shrubs, in addition to the rocks. Almost certainly an illustration of Euripides' lost tragedy *Andromeda,* with clear indications of setting: but not all of these figures would have been in front of the audience at the same time, so it might be termed a composite picture. The parody of this play by Aristophanes in *Women at the Thesmophoria* reveals that there was an Echo in the cave behind Andromeda.

PLATE 6. A Sicilian wine-mixing bowl, of about 380 B.C. Again a composite picture, here of Euripides' late tragedy *Antiope.* Lycus and Dirce persecuted Antiope, and her sons took revenge on Dirce by tying her to a bull:

her death is pictured on the left, but would have been reported by a messenger. To the right Zethos and Amphion, the sons of Antiope, are shown about to kill Lycus. They are restrained by the god Hermes, who has appeared above on the *mechane*. Antiope runs away on the right. The painting (like plate 5) has clear indications of setting, in the rocks, trees, and the animal skin, and the climax of the play is shown taking place in the mouth of the cave that had been the home of Amphion and Zethos.

PLATE 7. A Greek cup (*skyphos*), from southern Italy, of about 350–325 B.C. The painting is of interest because it shows a female acrobat balancing on revolving wheel, one of the tricks described in the account given by Xenophon in his dialogue *Symposium* of an entertainment in a private house in Athens. The entertainment occurs at a drinking party that supposedly took place in the later fifth century B.C., while the vase painting is about a century later. The small ensemble in Xenophon's *Symposium* is owned by and under the direction of a Greek from Syracuse, and the vase painting seems to confirm that mixed acrobatic and dramatic performance continued to be popular in the Greek communities of southern Italy. Yet neither the acrobatics nor the performance in Xenophon's *Symposium* involve a masked and padded comic actor, the crouching figure pulling the cords that turn the wheel in this painting. These actors are, however, familiar from a whole series of vase paintings from southern Italy from the fourth century B.C., and their relationship to earlier Athenian drama has been discussed by O. Taplin, *Comic Angels,* Oxford, 1993.

GENERAL INDEX

Numbers in boldface type refer to principal treatments of the subject

Actors and performers, 9, 14, 21, 31, **34–38**, **60–64**, 69–73, 76, 77–78, 88; and chorus, 69–73; and comic costume, 28; and masks, 25–27; number of, 23, 26, 34–38; playwrights as, 16, 34, 37–38; and singing, 37–38, 74–75, 76; and tragic costume, 27–28

Aeschylus: and his actors, 37; as character in *Frogs,* 52, 76; his tragedies as an influence on Euripides, 79–80; his use of costume, 27–28; number of his plays, 6

Akropolis, 2, 17, 17, 64

Altars, 61, 70

Aristophanes: his revision of *Clouds,* 52; his use of costume and properties, 28–29; his use of parody, 29, 57–58, 74–79; his use of the scene building, 47; masks in his comedies, 26, 96; number of his plays, 6

Assembly, 50, 54, 58, 64; parody of its formulas in *Women at the Thesmophoria,* 78; on Pnyx hill, 46, 50

Athenian citizens, 9, 21, 49, 52, 74, 79; as *choregoi,* 9; as composers of plays, 2, 16. *See also* Assembly; Audience; Democracy

Athens, 2, 4, 17, 25, 30–31, 46, 50; immigrants in, 49; narrative painting in, 23; purchase of texts in, 76; worship of Dionysus at, 7–8, 25, 30–31

Attica, 8, 11, 77

Audience, 1–2, 8, 17, 37, **49–53**, 68, 70, 88, 88; addressed by characters or chorus, 32, 35, 36; and its reactions to performance, 15, 36, 52, 56, 59, 74; the modern, 85, 91; and parody, 77–81

Chants, 70, 73, 88

Choregos/-oi, 8, 14, 34

Chorus, 8, 16, 17, **30–33**, 36, 38, 46, 60, 61–62; and actors in comedy, 36–37, 63; and actors in early tragedy, 34; addressed by characters, 34, 46, 55–57; comic costumes for, 28; later decline of, 77–78; and leading character, 42; and the *Parabasis,* 32, 72; and physical action, 33, 63, 63–64, 68–73; and the playing space, 44–48; tragic masks and costumes for, 25–27. *See also* Dance; Songs and choral singing; Verse and meter

Citizens. *See* Athenian citizens

City Dionysia, 26, 37, 49; comedy and tragedy at, 31–32, 74; competition for actors at, 33–34; organization of, **8–9**; revivals at, 77. *See also* Audience; *Choregos/-oi;* Competitions; Festivals of Dionysus; Lenaea

Competitions, dramatic, 7–8, 15; for actors, 34, 36; judgment of, 52; prizes for actors in, 37; prizes for playwrights in, 14–15, 34

Composition of plays, 14–15, 33–34; affected by audience reaction, 52; and delivery by the actor, 57; and messenger speeches, 58–59; skills required of playwright for, 14. *See also* Songs and choral singing

Costume, 1, 9, **28–29**; changing of, 20, 34; comic, 28, 32; in comic parody, 75–76; elaboration of, 28; range of, 40; for the satyr play, 28–29; tragic, 27–28; in worship of Dionysus, 26

Dance: choral, 14, 31, 65, 69, 71, 88; in early Greek communities, 30; in the early *orchestra,* 17; in satyr plays, 33, 76; training for playwright in, 15, 16; in worship of Dionysus, 7

Delivery, **54–59**, 88

Democracy, 8, 49–50, 52; importance of public speaking in, 49–50; parody of its institutions, 78

Dialogue, 12, 34; its importance in comedy, 36

Didaskalos, 14, 31

Dionysus: as character in *The Bacchae,* 26; as character in *Frogs,* 60, 76–77; as character in private performance, 13; choruses in honor of, 30–31; and the dithyramb, 7; festivals of, 7–8, 10; *mainades* as followers of, 7; masks in worship of, 7, 28, 30–31; precinct of, 17, 20–21; processions in honor of, 31;

78; satyrs as followers of, 7, 33; worship of, 7, 28, 30–31

Direction, theatrical, 14, 57

Distortion, 25; in comic masks, 26; as technique of comedy, 52, 59, 74, 78

Dithyramb. *See under* Dionysus

Ekkuklema, 20–21, 47, 60, 70; in comic parody, 75, 76

Epidaurus, ancient theater at, 22, 85

Euripides: as character in comedies by Aristophanes, 52, 57, 75, 76; and comedy, 79; his approach to tragedies by Aeschylus, 79–80; his use of costume, 27–28; his use of masks, 26–27; his work parodied by Aristophanes, 27, 29, 74–75, 79; number of his plays, 6

Festivals, 30

Festivals of Dionysus: local dramatic, 8, 77–78; organization of, **7–9**; rural, 46; and the theater, 2, 17–22, 49, 70. *See also* City Dionysia; Lenaea

Fragments of plays, 6, 75

Homer, composer of the *Iliad* and *Odyssey,* 5, 81

Lenaea, 8, 37, 74

Masks, **25–27**, 36, 85; changing of, 20, 34; comic, 26; and mask makers, 26, 58; in mime, 12; for the satyr play, 28; set of, 40; tragic, 25–27, 62; in the worship of Dionysus, 7, 31

Mechane, 21, 29, 74–75

Menander, 5; absence of a choral script in his comedies, 32; his characters, 15; rediscovery of his work, 5; the scene building in his comedies, 45, 47

Messenger speeches, 58–59

Mime, 12–13

Music, 14, 16, 30, 65–66, 68, 76, 88
Myth, 5, 15, 33, 66, 76

Neurospastos, 10, 13

Olympian gods, 7; Aphrodite, 66–68;
    Apollo, 29, 30–31, 60, 70; Artemis, 29,
    30–31; Athene, 70; Zeus, 61. *See also*
    Dionysus
Orchestra, 17, 44–47; and choral action,
    69–73; in the *agora*, 17; shape of, 22

Parabasis. See under Chorus
Parody, 29, 57, **74–81**
Pericles, 9, 22
Piraeus, 8, 77
Plato, on puppets in *Republic* and *Laws*,
    10–11
Playing space, 1, 17–22, **44–48**, 60–64,
    68–73
Pnyx. *See under* Assembly
Properties, 25, 27, **29**, 32, 40, 46, 71, 75
Puppets, 10–11, 13

Reading of playtexts, 39–43; and adapta-
    tion, 88–88; ancient, 76–77; modern,
    1, 53, 60, 67–68; translations designed
    for, 85
Religion, 30, 57, 68, 69, 79, 90–91; Sopho-
    cles and, 16
Revivals of plays: ancient, 8, 77–78; mod-
    ern, 86, 91; in modern adaptations,
    85–88, 90–91
Roles: allocation of, 35–36, 58; and
    masks, 26–27
Routines, comic, 36, 63

Satyrs and satyr plays, 6, 9, 15, 33, 68,
    70; and adaptation, 82; composers of,
    5; costumes for, 28–29; illustrations
    of, 28–29; and parody, 76; and
    Silenus, 28–29; theatrical settings
    for, 21–22

Scene building, **17–22**, 35, 44; as cave, 24,
    46, 52–53; doors of, 20, 21, 23, 44–48,
    53, 60, 63, 69–70; as palace, 24, 53, 60–
    61, 61–62; in performance, 44–48, 54,
    56, 60–64, 69–71; roof of, 20, 47, 63,
    79; and scenography, **23–24**; social
    implications of, 53; as temple, 24, 45,
    53, 60–61, 70; as tent, 20, 24, 53, 60–
    61; used to change masks and cos-
    tumes, 20, 27, 35; used to define set-
    ting, 44–48
Scenography. *See under* Scene building
Sicily, 12
Silenus. *See under* Satyrs and satyr plays
Skene. See Scene building
Socrates, 26, 58, 63, 78
Songs and choral singing, **30–33**, **65–73**;
    in combination with actors, 35, 72–
    73; in the comedies of Menander, 32,
    45; composed by the playwright, 14–
    15; presenting problems for modern
    translators, 88–90; in the worship of
    Dionysus, 7, 17
Sophocles: and his actors, 38; his biogra-
    phy, 16; his tragedies as an influence
    on Euripides, 80; his use of proper-
    ties, 29; number of his plays, 6
Sophron, 10, 13
Symposium, 12–13
Syracuse, 12–13

Theater of Dionysus, 2, 4, 7, **17–22**, 44
Theatron, 17, 21, 49. *See also* Audience
Thespis, 31, 34
Translations, 1, 39, 72, **82–92**
Trilogy, definition of, 8

Vase paintings, 1, 24, 26–29, 32–33, 37
Verse and meter, 14, 34, 65–68, 88–90

Women: and the audience, 49; excluded
    as performers, 38; in myth, as follow-
    ers of Dionysus, 7, 28

Women characters: choral portrayal of, 64, 69–71, 72; in comic parody, 74–75; male actors' portrayal of, 36, 38, 54–55, 57, 60–61, 64, 64, 79; in parody of male institutions, 78; represented in choral action, 64, 78; represented in choral song, 66–68; represented by mask and costume, 26–28. See also *Women at the Thesmophoria* in Index of Plays

Xenophon, on private performance in *Symposium,* 10, 12–13

INDEX OF PLAYS

Ae. = Aeschylus
Ar. = Aristophanes
Eu. = Euripides
So. = Sophocles

Acharnians (Ar.), 28, 29, 31, 46, 58, 63, 71,
    75, 76, 77, 78, 79
Agamemnon (Ae.), 42, 46, 54–55, 82–85, 89
Ajax (So.), 24, 76
Alcestis (Eu.), 36
Andromache (Eu.), 27
Andromeda (So.), 37
Andromeda and *Antiope* (Eu., lost
    tragedies), 24, 74, 75, 77
Antigone (So.), 41, 42, 56–57, 80

The Bacchae (Eu.), 26, 28, 68, 69, 79, 80
Birds (Ar.), 24, 28, 48, 73, 76, 78, 79

Clouds (Ar.), 28, 32, 52, 58, 63, 79
Cyclops (Eu.), 33, 81

Electra (Eu.), 24, 80
Electra (So.), 29, 55
Eumenides (Ae.), 44, 69–70, 72

Frogs (Ar.), 27, 28, 48, 52, 60, 75, 76, 77,
    80, 91

Hecuba (Eu.), 27, 60
Helen (Eu.), 24, 26–27, 44, 57, 71, 74, 79
Heracles (Eu.), 46, 60
Hippolytus (Eu.), 61, 66–68, 87

Ion (Eu.), 41, 45, 60–61
Iphigenia at Aulis (Eu.), 80
Islands (Ar.), 32

Knights (Ar.), 32, 58, 78

Libation Bearers (Ae.), 36, 73, 80
Lysistrata (Ar.), 42, 48, 64, 72, 76, 78, 91

Medea (Eu.), 29, 36, 41, 55, 61

Oedipus at Colonus (So.), 36, 41, 61–62
Oedipus the King (So.), 27, 41, 61, 80
Orestes (Eu.), 79

Peace (Ar.), 29, 47, 48, 75, 78
The Persians (Ae.), 27, 35, 44, 69
Philoctetes (So.), 24, 45, 62
The Phoenician Women (Eu.), 80

Seven against Thebes (Ae.), 35, 69, 80
The Suppliant Maidens (Ae.), 35, 69
Suppliant Women (Eu.), 70, 72, 80

Telephos (Eu., lost tragedy), 75–76, 77
Thamyras (So., lost tragedy), 37–38
Transport Ships (Ar., lost play), 28, 32
Trojan Women (Eu.), 27, 87

Wasps (Ar.), 28, 29, 42, 47, 63, 76, 78, 79
Women at the Thesmophoria (Ar.), 48, 57–58, 66, 72, 74, 75, 76, 78, 79
Women in Assembly (Ae.), 47, 48, 64, 78
Women of Trachis (So.), 29, 58, 68